Timmy the Timid, Timmy the Tender

TIMMY THE TIMID
TIMMY THE TENDER

TOOLS FOR COPING WITH GRIEF

Patricia McClaflin Booher

Rock Pavilion Press

Also books written by Patricia McClaflin Booher

Beloved Homeland, "Growing up on a Wyoming Homestead"

Reflections of a Wyoming Shepherd on the 23rd Psalm

Soon to be released

Creativity, "Beauty Unfolding"

Here Lamby, Lamby, Lamby

Lessons of Life I Learned in my Garden Patch

Copyright © Patricia McClaflin-Booher

ROCK PAVILION PRESS

www.patriciamac.com

All rights reserved. No part of this book may be reproduced or transmitted in any form or by any means, electronic or mechanical, including photocopying, recording, or by any information storage and retrieval system without the written permission of the Publisher, except where permitted by law.
    For information address: Rock Pavilion Press.

Book Cover Design: John Booher (Grandson)

All Scripture quotations are taken from the Holy Bible, New King James Version, NKJV. Copyright 1982 and New International Version, NIV. Copyright 1978

Printed in the United States of America

DEDICATION

Craig and Sandy Booher

Paul and Shana Lewis

Mitch and Rachel Ross

All along the way in this life of a writer, there have been those walking closely beside me. There were times when Mom was raw with emotion in the writing and the daunting task seemed overwhelming. In each instance my children and their mates cheered me on in so many ways. This gave me courage to keep climbing up the mountain side and for that my life is blessed.

Ask of Me, and I will give You
The nations for Your inheritance.
And the ends of the earth for Your possession.
Psalm 2:8 NKJV

TABLE OF CONTENTS

INTRODUTION	1
SECTION I: Once upon a time there was a dog named Timmy.	7
Chapter 1: Time to Say Good-By	9
Tribute to Timmy	11
Death Comes in Many Forms	14
Chapter 2: Some Things are Just a Mystery that do not need an answer	19
Monday Morning is coming	22
Letter to the Veterinarian	26
Chapter 3: The Origin of Timmy	31
Canine Friends	34
Timmy Comes on the Scene	37
Katie Disappears	38
Wyoming 4-H Family	39
Chapter 4: In the Garden	45
SECTION II: And then there is grief and how to survive it.	55
Chapter 5: Five Stages of Grief	57
Denial	58
Anger	59
Tame the Tiger	59
Death of a Parent	62
Bargaining	65
Depression	67
Robes of Comfort	69
Acceptance	70
Maple Leaves, Lemon Balm and Exposed Roots	71
Chapter 6: Thankfulness	77
White Wool, Beads and Silk Ribbon Flowers	80
When the Little Things Become the Big Stuff	83
Chapter 7: Forgiveness	89
The Butterfly Bush	90

4-H Sheep Tragedy	98
Chapter 8: Humor:	107
How is the Elastic in Your PJs?	108
Chapter 9: Creativity	113

SECTION III: Everyone has a story. — 119

Chapter 10: Cup Half Full/Cup Half Empty/Your Choice	121
Cream of the Crop	122
Stages of Life	124
Choices	129
Chapter 11: Grief and Trauma	131
Chapter 12: Deep Calls to Deep	141
Chapter 13: Car Wreck in Shirley Basin	149
Chapter 14: The Silent Lessons from my Garden	159
Chapter 15: Empty Flower Pots	167
Chapter 16: The Blighted Petals of Life	177
Chapter 17: Cups of Prayer	185

SECTION IV: Light at the end of the tunnel. — 193

Chapter 18: The Sun Did Come up Today	195
Sparrows and Crows	197
Sunrise in Winter	200
Chapter 19: Cotton Balls in the Sky	207

SECTION 5: Moss covered flower pots made of clay. — 213

Chapter 20: Broken Flower Pots	215
Chapter 21: Potters Hand	221
Robin Red Breast	224
Passing on the Baton	233
REFERENCES	236
BOOK ORDER INFORMATION	238

INTRODUCTION

As you pick up this book with the little Yorky dog Timmy howling in his excitement of friends coming to visit, you very likely are walking through your own grief. You might be giving this book on grief to a friend. Grief, regardless of the reason taps into all the senses of the human race as well as the animal kingdom. Some experiences of grief can blend into the journey and then we proceed to the next chapter. There are other aspects of grief where life will be forever changed, never to return to the past or the present.

At this time if you can only read one page or maybe a chapter that is okay. If you need to go directly to the last chapter feel free. If you are still numb at the loss you are walking through you might want to put this little book on the back shelf for a season.

In the previous books written, I spent a good deal of time bringing back to memory those who had been such an asset in bringing those books to completion. This will not be the case with this Timmy book, as the story spans a lifetime and beyond. I just want to say I am most grateful for all those dear hearts who have invested themselves into my life. In the periods of grief their love and friendship cannot be measured in earthly terms.

I will have to mention my editor, Robin Hoover-Niles. Her dedication and support during the completion of the book is incredible. It is my heart's desire to pass the baton to my grandchildren of writing down stories of life.

John Booher, my grandson, has designed the book cover. I am working with all the grandchildren in making the videos and blogs.

As you read through the chapters, you will find that they are not in chronological order. I have inserted snippets of my own journey from past experiences which have been dated.

I describe the day I became a writer as "the first day of the rest of my life." Those first poems written during a winter storm while living in my home in Shell, Wyoming are safely tucked away in a journal now yellow with age. That was in 1994, so I was not a young woman. If I would have had any idea that I would one day be an author, hopefully I would have paid closer attention in the English grammar class in grade school.

I share some stories from childhood, but mostly this non-fiction narrative of Timmy began in Shell Wyoming. We then came to our old vintage home in Michigan where the Wyoming Shepherd was written. My next home was in an apartment where the "Lessons of Life I learned in my Garden Patch" was written. In this season of my life's journey I am blessed to be looking out on the lake in the mornings watching the swans. It is a balm of soothing ointment to my soul as I am in the finishing stages of completing this book on grief.

One of the poems I wrote in that first writer's journal was "Deep Calls to Deep," Throughout my life journey I have gone back and read those words countless times, especially in those days of adversity or grief. What inspired that poem were the times when I needed a reprieve from the hectic, I would drive up to the Shell falls and just watch the torrents of water cascading down the mountain side and it would sooth my heart at times when it was aching.

When we are young with our childhood dreams it is not possible to plan ahead for those divergent paths in which the streams of life can take us. At times the river flows steady with no unexpected tributaries. But then the flash flood comes and it can wash away all those dreams of childhood, leaving one bewildered, and the unwanted companion can come along side and its name is grief.

Early on as a writer, I attended a Writer's Conference in Jackson Hole, Wyoming. I kept low key as I was just in the beginning stages of writing. I wish I could remember the name of one of the morning speakers as she made an indelible impression on me. She was an accomplished author. She said, "We write because we have to write." Then she added, "When you have achieved your goal as a successful author, you in turn have to give back."

During the book tour in in the summer of 2009 with "Reflections of a Wyoming Shepherd on the 23rd Psalm," it was always a delight when a young person would come up and tell me they wanted to be a writer. Some of the most treasured years of my life were when I was a teacher, but that will always be with me, as it still brings me great delight to teach a skill of any kind to others.

Those hours I spent flying home from my mother's funeral, I knew I would have to complete the "Beloved Homeland" book no matter what. That would require me to retire from my work with Sam's Club as it would demand all my energy. It felt like I was stepping right off one of those Big Horn Mountain cliffs, but I did it! And then Covid came along, as an unwanted guest.

It is at times like this I go back and thank my homestead parents, as they gave me true grit and endurance to just keep climbing.

Actually, it was a relief that I was in lock-down, as the process of getting the book ready for publication took every fiber of endurance I had in me. What a joy it was the day I received my first copy of "Beloved Homeland" in the mail.

As months went by and I heard of the elderly locked away from family and many times dying alone, I knew I had to get out the manuscript of "Timmy" and finish writing and getting it published. I would think of the process of walking through those stages of grief of my own mother passing away while designing the wool dress. Our family was together that week before her funeral, as each one of us took part in planning every detail. It was a beautiful funeral service as family and friends were there to share the amazing life of this mother so loved.

I had finished the homestead book and then the process of moving from the apartment took a big chunk of time. I tried to be ever so careful as I surely did not want to come down with Covid, but it did happen and I had a heavy dose of the virus. There were months of recovery and I still have lingering fatigue and mind fog so it has slowed me down, but day after day I pray for strength and write as long as I dare. I will admit that in walking through that time of illness, it has added a layer of compassion as I write the final chapters of this narrative.

In the planning stages of writing this book on grief, I wanted to limit the size of the manuscript. I have briefly spoken of some research that has been helpful to me throughout my career and personal life. You will find quotes throughout the chapters. References can be found on the last pages. I briefly refer to four tools in coping with grief but there are many more.

You might have picked up this little book as you have a friend or family member you want to come along side and be that empathic listener. Sometimes in our desire to help that one we care so much about, we ask too many questions. In trying to ease the pain we try and give an answer for the tragedy, which only makes it worse. How often has it been said, "Oh I know just how you feel." Really, how can we ever know just how another person is feeling?

I will go back to a personal memory I have that I will always cherish. Our family came back to Michigan after my father's funeral. I just could not imagine how I would ever be able to come to grips with never seeing that smile that would light up my Daddy's face when I would be able to come home to Wyoming.

It was that first Sunday back in church. I was down in front of the sanctuary, just wishing I could run away to somewhere private. Roy Crossman was a dear man who always said I was just like one of his daughters. He came up, put his strong arms around me and held me. I laid my head on his shoulder and we wept. He did not say a word but I will never forget his empathic heart.

Each time I come to the last editing I find myself questioning how the story has evolved into completion. This narrative truly has woven throughout my life so there are consistencies of my story that seem to repeat over and over. I could go back and delete parts of stories, but then I remember when I wrote each snippet of my journey those were the emotions I was experiencing at the time. I trust as you read of those simple but profound everyday experiences that brought me faith and courage in times of grief you will be encouraged in your own journey.

So dear one, may I come along side and walk ever so gently with you. My deepest desire and prayer is that as you read through these snippets of life with the elements of every day happenings you will take on hope and comfort.

SECTION I

ONCE UPON A TIME THERE WAS A DOG
NAMED TIMMY

CHAPTER 1

TIME TO SAY GOOD-BY

As I look back on that early morning standing there on the deck, I had no idea what was about to take place. The sun was only a tiny sliver in the eastern sky with heavy dew dripping from the trees below. It was a relief that the morning still had a bit of chill as very soon the August heat would press down on my spirit. It had been a restless night of sleep. As I stood there peering down through the iridescent leaves of green I saw the small violet colored mums amongst the rocks and it brought some relief to my broken heart.

I had no idea on that morning that in just a few days a story would begin to take form. The main character in this story will be Timmy. The title, "Timmy the Timid, Timmy the Tender," was easy to decide as it is a perfect picture of this little Yorky/Pomeranian and who knows what else kind of dog. He is now wrapped in a small green flannel baby blanket with a lamb sewn in the corner. He is resting out in the garden where I can see his grave from my window. There are heavy slate stones lying over the grave to protect him. I planted a violet colored mum plant next to his grave. Every morning I would carry a watering can down and water the flowers and the slate rocks over the grave.

This world of writing has become my muse. Well I should say one of many. Quilting is the hands on of color that brings such a sense of creativity that blesses my life.

The hot cinnamon rolls I have made forever are an everyday kind of activity. Not such a big deal to me, but my neighbors and grandchildren would have something else to say about that one. As you will recognize from the snippets of stories gardening and the forest creatures are another part of my life and now I have added the lake view.

I am well aware by this season of writing that the story at some point seems to take on a life of its own. There are other stories pushing me hard in the background. I am realizing the ink needs to dry from the last word penned in this story of my little dog Timmy.

I hope the picture taken one day in my upstairs office while writing the "Beloved Homeland" book will be on the cover. We will see how that works out. Whenever friends would come Timmy would remember. Even if he had not seen them for a long time he would be so full of joy that he would run to them and howl and howl until they would pet his little head. Timmy was a one person dog but he still made room for the grandchildren. In all the family pictures he is right in the middle of them. He only weighed about five pounds and as he got older, I am sure his little bones would ache.

He had many funny antics which would bring me delight. I am not sure how much my friends enjoyed his habits, but out of love for me they would go along. My friends Mary Ellen and Carol would say they didn't like dogs, but Timmy didn't care about that. In those early mornings out in the sunroom, he would always nestle down under his quilt next to me as I said my prayers and prepared for a day of writing.

When Mary Ellen would come he would transfer over to her lap, and this would always make me laugh.

I knew in time she also came to love this little Yorky type.

The thoughts of writing this type of book had never occurred to me until a few days after Timmy's death. I had tried for ever so long to prepare myself, as he was so old and sick. But isn't that the way it is when we have a loved one. We know from the time we are very young that one day we will bury our parents. For those of us who are parents, we hope and pray it is not in the reverse. When the time came that summer on a hot Thursday morning in August, I was numb with grief. I couldn't call anyone and yet this little pet had made his way into the hearts of so many friends, I knew they would want to know. By Friday afternoon, I had to do something with this grief, as so many times in the past I sat down and wrote a "Tribute to Timmy."

Timmy had been my pet for eighteen long years and we had traveled through hill and dale together down through the years. So many friends had come to love this little pet of mine, so I knew I would need to contact them. I sent out the "Tribute to Timmy" letter to close friends and posted his picture and letter on Facebook.

TRIBUTE TO TIMMY

For you, my precious friends who have walked out this journey of life, and have loved me so well, I wanted to share with you, but right now the sorrow is deep so I chose my best mode of communication in this season of life, and that is writing.

Yesterday morning with my daughter Shana holding me in her arms, Timmy slipped away. He was eighteen. Wow, what an amazing little dog that has graced my life through so many valleys and mountain tops.

I have often thought of the goodness of our Heavenly Shepherd who would design this connection between those of us pet lovers and the capacity of unconditional love the animal kingdom can possess for their human family.

I do believe Timmy has sat at my feet throughout the years of writing every poem, every chapter of books, and snippets of life. As you well know, I write from that deep place in my soul and spirit, so many times before the writing came, there would be tears of anguish and then I would put my hands on the keyboard and write with passion.

I think Timmy had become deaf and blind in the end, slept a great deal, but just until the last while, when you would come to my home you were met with my little doggy howling and barking for joy. Thus, I wanted to share this memory of my little pet who loved all my friends, children and grandchildren so well.

After the wreck in Shirley Basin in Wyoming, life was never the same for me, as it was a miracle I survived it. In those months following, of course I was in a great deal of pain, and didn't know if I could ever work again, but I was just so full of joy that I would see another spring so I was never sad. Many days I felt just an overwhelming need to pray those deep prayers and would have to walk around my home. Timmy always knew when I prayed, so if I didn't pick him up, he would get on the back of the couch, put his paw out, and the remainder of the time praying he would snuggle down in my arms and be carried around.

I could go on and on with stories of this amazing little dog, but will close in thanking the Shepherd of Heaven that he would send me such an amazing little friend who has been so close to my heart.

I must now get through the grief of it all, by turning my sorrow into loving others, as that is what is so needed in these serious times we live in. God Bless each of you who have loved me so well throughout my journey.

Timmy died, August 21, 2014

The next few days, although the grief was so deep in my heart, I began to read the comments on Facebook. I quit counting after about eighty-five. I was so taken with the kindness expressed to me, but also deep pain of others in their own loss.

I will describe the importance of my little garden out there in front of my apartment in a later chapter but for now I will try to explain, to you the reader, the beautiful thing that has come out of this time of grief for my beloved little pet.

The night time seemed to be the hardest for me. My sleep was fitful as I would wake up crying. I have neighbors above and below me and I didn't want them to hear me cry so I would get up, put on my robe and walk down to the garden. This would happen usually around four in the morning, when the world was silent and everyone else was asleep. I stood on the edge of the garden where the flood lights would catch my silhouette.

I was relieved that Timmy could now be at rest, as in the end he was so sick, but I just missed him terribly as he had been with me all those years of writing the books and poems. He would sit at my feet hour after hour just waiting to crawl up in my lap.

It is complicated trying to explain about this silent voice of God to others, but that is how I do hear or know God is speaking to me.

Night after night I would go to my garden down below my deck. I knew this could not continue as I had a busy schedule of work during the day. I knew I had to get a grip on the time of grief.

One night as I wept over Timmy's grave that silent voice began to speak to me, "I have something I want you to write for me." My thoughts came back with a touch of despair, "How can I write without Timmy right there beside me, as he has always been my gentle comfort?" The silent voice spoke again. "If you will just trust me, more than you ever have, I will fill your mind and thoughts with the words and you will come to love me in deeper ways than ever in the past." In the next few days the thoughts did come to me and I would have to say I was in awe as I realized I would be writing on this emotion called grief and all would be well with my soul.

DEATH COMES IN MANY FORMS
In the ebb and flow of life, the river can make many turns, some expected and then there are those that come upon one, sometimes with sorrow. When the channel of water turns into death most often grief will be the partner.

From the time we are young, we have in the back part of living, the knowledge that one day we will say good-bye to our parents. When the new born is placed in our arms, there is a deep desire that we will go first but this is not always the case.

For those of us who open our hearts to loving a pet, what a risk we take. As I have just come through the process of having my little pet, for ever so long now, I do feel a portion of Heaven has opened in my heart as I look back at the joy and peace that Timmy has graced my life with.

As the days of sorrow have slipped into that place when I can reflect I think of those small details that had troubled me, such as where he would be buried, would he die in the night next to me, when would it happen, would I be away, which was troubling to me; on and on the questions would go.

When it comes to saying good-by, the visual picture of the family all around the bedside in unity with a parent slipping away without pain is what we hope for. Unfortunately, suffering many times is a companion of death. This body we have been given can break, accidents can happen; ravages of disease can take a long time, leaving the family to grope with the memories that can haunt the soul for some time.

I would say the hardest situation is when death comes because of evil done to another. This last summer has been difficult and each day the magnitude of evil seems to reach further from its source. Societies across the globe have had to witness the beheading of innocent victims. Down through the ages, there have been such happenings, but with the Internet a part of daily life, we are quickly propelled to the darkest places.

As I would awake early in the last few months, in my quiet time of prayer my heart was drawn to those parents of those small children who were being decapitated.

Knowing that very soon I would hold my pet for the last time, it would be easy to say it wasn't important, compared to the atrocities across continents. There is something about the unconditional love that is given from a pet that somehow helps in this journey of life.

I would say as my own journey has had many unexpected turns and sometimes it brought great sorrow, as I learned to fall back into the arms of this great Shepherd of Heaven, I found the grief would take on a fragrance of beauty, which only could come from the hand of a Savior, who himself suffered more then we in our human frame can comprehend.

As I speak for myself, I will have to say this has been an amazing journey in writing this little book on "Coping with Grief." There have been times in the past while writing; I would experience sorrow but not this time. I was surprised at times I didn't feel sad but rather my emotions were raw. Parts of the Timmy book I will share with you, the reader, are snippets of my own journey. At other times I will direct you to resources that have aided me in my seasons of living and loving, winning and losing.

I am surprised at some of those portions of my journey I am sharing. As I look back over this life journey I have walked, I have experienced grief. More than that I have had such a rich life filled with goodness and family and friends. In my own gentle way of writing, I have the opportunity to share with you and come along side and give you an encouraging word.

I think I need to explain at this point of the story; I have tried as best I could to put the chapters in chronological order but that will not always be the case in this story. From the beginning of my writing life, I always had a sense that I needed to date the poems and stories, so you will see that as I have compiled this little book, I have woven portions into the manuscript that have given me courage, sometimes when I wondered if I would make it through my own grief.

So let us begin this journey together. For you the reader, if you find yourself in that season when your heart is broken in grief, as you read down through the contents and topics, you might just want to read one portion. That is just fine, as right now you might not be able to take in too much information. You will note, I have included resources that have been beneficial in the past. I will not go into great detail, but rather wanted to make you, the reader, aware.

CHAPTER 2

SOME THINGS ARE JUST A MYSTERY

THAT DO NOT NEED AN ANSWER

Down through the years of my own journey of life there have been some of those old hymns I have come across, many times in those grieving times. After the afternoon of my family helping bury my little pet Timmy, I had to regroup as it was the last night my oldest grandson would be home. He was in training at the time with the Air Force and stationed in San Diego. As I drove out to my son Craig's home that evening I prayed for strength just to keep my composure.

We would not see Erik again for a year, so I just had to somehow pull myself together. I usually never leave my keys in the car but that night I did. I managed to get through my visit without crying, although I knew Erik, insightful young man that he is, knew I was having a hard time. When I walked out to my car the lights were on. That was a puzzle, but more than that, when I got into the car, the keys were on, and the battery was dead. How frustrating, as by now I just wanted to go home. My son-in-law, Paul came out and tried to start the car, but it was difficult. Craig drove up and came over. I said, "Craig this is the worst day of my life." Well of course that was not true, but in sorrow we do say some things like that don't we?

My family got me on my way and as I drove down the road I was surprised that the radio was on and old hymns were playing.

When I got to the stop sign I looked to see what station was on and realized it was a CD I didn't even know was in the car. I sat there for a few minutes trying to collect my thoughts, wondering why I would leave the keys on, as that was a first for me, and then realized I did not have the radio or CD player on when I arrived.

I did listen to those wonderful old hymns all the way home and for the next few weeks until the storm passed over.

A few days later I was telling my sister Pam about what had happened, just trying to figure out why the car and CD player were on. With insight she spoke these words to me, "Patty don't question how it happened; just count it as a mysterious blessing". That is just what I have done, for as the days passed and the melodies of God's love and faithfulness went down into my soul and spirit, a thankful heart emerged at knowing the blessing of so many years and of the countless beautiful memories that had graced my life. As days passed into weeks, the sorrow of my heart turned into words that would be penned as I would ponder on this mighty God of the universe who would have on his mind the details of bringing this little dog into my life.

O the Deep, deep Love of Jesus

Oh, the deep, deep love of Jesus
Vast, unmeasured, boundless, free
Rolling as a mighty ocean
In its fullness over me

Underneath me, all around me
Is the current of Thy love
Leading onward, leading homeward
To Thy glorious rest above

Oh, the deep, deep love of Jesus
Deeper than the deepest sea
The love that led my Christ to die
Is the love that set me free

Oh, the deep, deep love of Jesus
Spread His praise from shore to shore
How He's loving, ever loving
Changing never, never more

How He watches over His loved ones
Died to call them all His own
How for them He's interceding
Watching over them from the throne

Oh, the deep, deep love of Jesus
Deeper than the deepest sea
The love that led my Christ to die
Is the love that set me free

Oh, the deep, deep love of Jesus
Love of every, love the best
It's an ocean vast of blessing
It's a haven sweet of rest

Oh, the deep, deep love of Jesus
It's a heaven of heavens to me
And it lifts me up to glory

For it lifts me up to Thee

Oh, the deep, deep love of Jesus
Deeper than the deepest sea
The love that led my Christ to die
Is the love that set me free
That set me free

Samuel Trevor Francis, 1834-1925

MONDAY MORNING IS COMING

If we live long enough, it is hoped that we do learn some lessons of life along the way. I have found that remembering specific dates of grief such as a parent dying has not been a profitable strategy of coping for me. It only brings on sadness and a lingering grief process that needs to pass into the next phase of living.

And so now I am reminding myself that lingering on that Thursday morning in late August when I was awake long before the sun would move up and over the eastern sky would only prolong the agony of walking through this little Timmy death.

Grief is a part of life. In some form or another each of us humans will find those times we do walk through this emotion. For those of us who love our pets, it is almost frightening to recognize how much they become a family member. The role of our pet plays in the everyday goings on in the family for the most part is taken for granted. If you are the faithful family member who takes the pictures of those events like birthdays, holidays and so forth; the pet usually finds his way into all the pictures with a smile on his face.

My little pet Timmy had been with me ever so long. Eighteen years is a duration that out lives most pets. That is just how long my life was blessed with Timmy. He was with me in the deep valleys and the high mountain top adventures.

I am the down in the soul writer. I describe those days of writing when I write like the wind, and in those moments in time my emotions are in the raw. I am well aware that snippets of stories in this little book will not be written without sorrow, but for those of us who have a heart for writing, we write because we have to write.

One morning as I was drinking my first cup of coffee, I recollected the phrase, "Monday morning quarterback." One of those simple pleasures of this age of the Internet is that right at our finger tips we can look up a multitude of things. The definition that most describes my thoughts this morning is this one.

Monday morning quarterback:
Noun, Informal, A person who criticizes the actions or decisions of another after the act, using hindsight to assess situations and specify alternative solutions.

If by chance you are in the stages of grief from losing a pet, maybe your spouse of fifty some years, or hopefully you are not walking through the sorrows of losing a child I pray the next paragraphs will be a solace to you.

How we handle grief and sorrow is such an individual process. There is no right or wrong way. Grief is just a part of life in the seasons we walk through.

The compassionate and understanding friend or family member is of priceless value in these times. As I look back over my own journey in life, there have been times that I was profoundly disappointed when sharing with that person I trusted, and then to realize they were not interested or couldn't deal with my grief which left me feeling desperately alone and even foolish.

I am not talking about using grief as manipulation. I am speaking of that true sorrow at the loss we experience when we deeply love a pet, family member or life circumstances that can bring sorrow and grief.

The Monday morning quarterback, who is quick to criticize, is no help during the process of walking through grief. Unfortunately sometimes the quarterback is that person you look at in the mirror on Monday morning. Unless you are using your grief to punish yourself, I don't know that any of us wants to linger in this process for an extended period.

One of those very tender blessings for me was the role my brother Wayne and his wife Pam played as my pet was dying. They also had a pet that was the great joy of their lives. Scooby was a special pug who watched TV and really did have the most charming personality.

I was still living in Wyoming when they brought Scooby home. I captured those first puppy pictures but never seemed to learn a good way to store pictures on my computer so I could find them quickly later. The morning Scooby died was filled with such sorrow. I searched for hours knowing I had to find the pictures and get them sent off in the mail as by now I was living in Michigan.

I would say it is not so much what we do, but the fact that we care for that other person's loss and allow ourselves to take on the vulnerable place of empathy in sharing with them.

I had been sharing for weeks with Pam early in the mornings of my sorrow over Timmy. I knew he was dying, but knowing he was so emotionally tied to me, I thought my pet would be so disappointed.

I prayed he would just die in his sleep. I don't recommend this, but my little Yorky had always slept with me. I would wake up countless times in the night checking on him, making sure he was covered up.

The Shepherd of Heaven knows each one of us far more then we know ourselves. That final morning came. Pam was saying, "Patty you can do this, you have to help Timmy." I called my daughter and she drove quickly across town. There was a vet just down the street. A grandpa type walked into the small office. I just wanted to hug him. Timmy slipped away in just a moment, but it seemed forever to me. I wrapped him up in his much loved quilt and my daughter drove me home. Later her husband Paul and my three grandsons came and we buried Timmy out next to the garden under the shadow of the maple tree. Paul covered the grave with heavy rocks and later I came back with some violet mums and planted them.

Over the next few days it seemed as if I was in a fog. I couldn't cry. In the night I kept waking up, reaching over to cover up Timmy, and then would remember he was gone. One night I had a terrible nightmare. It was so troubling that I got up out of bed, put on my robe and walked down to the garden. That was Sunday night but then Monday morning came and I cried.

In the weeks that followed when I prepared a meal I would forget for a moment and start to fix my little pet his snack. When I would come home from an exhausting day at work, and would walk into my apartment there was no little pet to greet me. I finally had to put all Timmy's items out of sight.

After a couple of weeks I finally got up enough courage to take my little shepherd book with a letter enclosed to the vet's office. I just wanted to do something to let the staff know how much I had appreciated their kindness to me. The old gentlemen vet was not there that afternoon, but the receptionist who had been there that morning remembered me. I tried to explain my thoughts of not wanting to disappoint my pet. I will always hold on to what she said to me. "Our pets don't want to disappoint their masters either so they just hold on."

September 4, 2014

FOR THE STAFF AT CLINTON TRAIL HOSPITAL

It has been two weeks since I came into your clinic with my daughter and beloved little Yorky type Timmy. I am writing this letter to you as the gratitude I have cannot really be adequately explained in words. In this season of my life, I write. It is a blessing but also a great coping skill that has seen me through some crushing and also joyous life situations.

I am thinking of the Bible story of the ten lepers who Jesus walked by. They cried out to him and he stopped on his journey and healed them all that day. But we read only one came back to thank him.

We come to you with our pets, many times only once when they are near death and I am sure not many return. I have grieved more than I dare admit for this precious little friend of eighteen years who has been with me through all the writing and loving grandchildren.

I am so grateful that my daughter Shana came with me, as I don't think I could have driven the car home or watched Timmy die. He is now out on the edge of the forest and I have planted scarlet colored mums that are beautiful at his grave. I cannot linger in this time of grief too long as the beautiful stories of his life are coming in the early predawn hours when it is completely quiet as I water his grave.

Timmy was so close to me and felt all my moods. I thought he should die in my arms, but the Shepherd of Heaven, in his wisdom knew, I would be haunted, so you were so close that morning when I knew he could no longer suffer.

You were so kind to me and for that I will always be thankful. It would be easy for you to take this daily business as mundane, but for each family who has loved their pet as a family member, your kindness will be indelibly printed on their hearts for a lifetime.

So thank you for being here for me and my pet. My children and grandchildren thank you as well. It hurts them to see Grandma now, but I will bounce back and the stories will be penned to the page to give another traveler courage to go on and smile again.

Most Sincerely,
Patricia Booher

I knew Timmy would not let go. What is this unconditional love of a pet? It is a mystery we just cannot comprehend. Of course there is a great price to pay in having that faithful pet at our side forever so long. When they slip away in death the price has a label and it is called grief.

We often hear the term, "Time heals all wounds." Well I would have to say, "Not exactly true." I came through that time and who would have believed that out of my own journey with this little Yorky dog that I would be writing to you as you are walking through your own journey of grief.

I have so many precious memories of that little dog. I knew I needed to give myself a wide berth before even thinking of having another pet. I have spoken to others who have also lost a pet and they never want to go through the pain again, so have chosen to not open that door.

Well right now I have a picture of a little white puppy right next to me as I write. He is nothing like Timmy and that is good. His name is Bezoo and already this happy little dog is conjuring up stories in my mind.

CHAPTER 3
THE ORIGIN OF TIMMY

I will briefly reflect on coming back to Wyoming after so many years. I accepted a position with the University of Wyoming Cooperative Extension. My first assignment was in Lincoln County. I found a chateau style home in Star Valley. It sat on four acres on a hillside that rose right up along the side of the mountain. The property was covered with Evergreen and Aspen trees.

I have so many stories I could tell of that short time, but that will come on another day. I would have to say this was the saddest time of my life. What comes to the top of the list of blessings for me in that time was the pet that would enter my life, and the close family friends that I would reunite with after many years.

I tell of the family, the Hoffs, in the "Beloved Homeland" book. It seemed to me in my childhood thoughts, if anything ever happened to my own mother and father, surely Bessie and Felix Hoff would become my second parents. Their daughter Phyllis, six years older than myself, I consider my big sister. When I was in the fourth grade, Melanie was born and then two years later Colleen came into our family group. They later sold their Paint Creek ranch and moved away to Idaho.

In the many seasons of life, there are many meandering streams that sometimes reconnect in a personal journey. I don't think this is by chance, especially in my own life circumstances.

Bessie passed away from a massive stroke several months after I had arrived back in Wyoming. I have wondered at times as I sat by her bedside if she could remember me.

Melanie's family and Felix lived just over the state line near Blackfoot, Idaho. I had to cross over mountain passes to go to the homestead, so there were many times I spent with their family and they in turn would come and enjoy my little home in the mountains.

One day Melanie called me with a suggestion. She knew the struggle in grief I was walking through so it was like a gift she handed me. She had a friend who needed to find a home for their old cocker spaniel. It had been the children's pet and now they had graduated and moved from home. The parents wanted to travel and Duchess was old and getting arthritis. Traveling would be very difficult for her.

I knew this would be a stretch to let myself love an old dog, plus I was required to travel a great deal with my job. Melanie said she would help out in those times. So here they came the next weekend with Duchess. What a wonderful pet she was. I think back on those times of weeping when she just patiently sat at my feet. There were many evenings we would take our stroll out through the woods looking out over the Swiss Alp type of mountain scenes.

We all decided to try cross-country skiing. Felix, way up in his eighties, even purchased skis. Looking back now, I wonder how wise we were. Duchess would faithfully follow along walking the path in the snow made by the skis. I am sure in the night hours her old bones ached, but she always had a smile on her face.

After a time I was transferred to Big Horn County Cooperative Extension.

I am a lover of the mountains, so once again I found a home in Shell, with a view looking right up into the Shell canyon, with the Big Horn mountain range looming over the eastern horizon.

It was during this time that I had back surgery. The surgeon said in no time I would be as good as new. Well that is not exactly how it all turned out. The blessing that came out of that down time is that I began to write. I just could not believe what I was penning to the page. I will speak more of this on the chapter on creativity, but Duchess was surely a comfort to me in those times when I was writing out my sorrow in poems and essays.

My daughter Shana came to live with me for a couple of years and brought her strange but wonderful little dog Buddy. Duchess was an old sage at adapting, so she put up with Buddy's antics as best she could. So now we had a pet family of two and then there were three.

The two Big Horn County Extension offices were in Basin and Lovell. I traveled back and forth through the week. My boss, Mike Schwope, like myself, loved dogs and horses and all animals. One afternoon when I was working in Lovell he called his friend Thelma to come over to the office.

When Thelma first brought the puppies into the Extension office, I stood firm. I did take time to play with the puppies and there was one that just stole my heart. I was required to travel a great deal, and my daughter did not need one more pet to look after when I was away.

I had already realized that a wedding would soon be approaching, so the care of these pets was going to be an obstacle I would have to find a way around. Mike and Thelma were determined. Thelma spoke up.

"That is no problem; whenever you have to be gone you can just bring your dogs to my house." She was a dog lover to the max. Well I managed to get through that visit and was careful not to mention it to my daughter that evening. I think the whole thing was a set up, so wouldn't you know, the next week when I was in Lovell working, here came Thelma, but this time she just had one puppy. I lost all sense of sanity that day holding that puppy.

The drive home to Shell was forty five miles from Lovell. All the way home I held that little bundle of fluff and fretted, "How am I going to tell my daughter what I have done?" I don't seem to recall too much difficulty as we both fell in love with this new family member and we named her Katie.

Duchess had been so patient with Buddy, and now here is this little puppy that wanted to play and wrestle around with her all day. Duchess would stand frozen in one spot, sometimes even showing her teeth, but after a few days, it was as if Katie had always been there. One evening after a long hard day at work, I made my nightly stroll to the garden down below the deck of the house. That evening I wrote one of my first little snippets of stories that would unfold through the years.

CANINE FRIENDS

As we ascend the small hill early in the evening after a day of demands, appointments, and deadlines, each of us feels an excitement. You see, this is our time of the day, reserved for the four of us.

There is Duchess; fourteen years old now, crippled with arthritis, very blind, and deaf as a doornail.

The family says I ought to put her to sleep. She's not good for anything; just put her out of her misery. But Duchess and I have this special bond. We have a private knowledge of life, even though age has a way of limiting us, life is rich and life is good.

Then there is Buddy. Now Buddy is another sort; a strange looking dog. Not sure what mother and father could come up with such a creature. He is very small, has curly gray hair, with teeth mostly all there, and each one crooked. There is something uncanny about Buddy. As he looks at you, one would have the feeling, he knows just how you feel. He is not an aggressive dog, but rather a passive gentle nature describes his whole outlook on life.

Katie came along last spring. Mind you, this home did not need another dog. No, Katie was accepted into our family purely by the fact she was a darling fluffy puppy that won my heart. At first she wasn't cuddly, had a terrible temper, and sent the other dogs into deep depression and a sense of loss. She had become center stage. She just moved right in and found her place, leaving them to shift around to accommodate her.

Katie and I had to sit down one day and have a heart to heart. You know what I mean, one of those talks that only those who have been blessed with an overwhelming out of control love for dogs type person has with any four legged creature that barks.

Well, anyway, we had our talk. I had to somehow help Katie understand that her adoption into this family basically only had one requirement.

She did not have to be smart. She did not have to be pretty. She did not have to have straight teeth. No, she did not even need to have a pedigree.

There was only one thing she did have to possess; to fit into this menagerie of canine and human. Her whole future in this family depended entirely on her willingness to become a floppsy, moppsy, lovable ball of fluff, willing at any time day or night to be picked up, rolled around and cuddled to almost the point of suffocation.

In a strange language known only to our kind, we commenced our discussion. Katie was a quick learner. She must have possessed wisdom far beyond her short life of just a few months. For lo and behold a new facet of Katie's personality began to unfold. Her short explosions of temper melted into a loving cuddly bundle of love. Although there were, and still are, remains of aggression and jealousy, the other sages of maturity have had to adjust as well.

It's one of those summer days that Wyoming is known for. Not a cloud in that deep blue sky. The air is so fresh and clean, along with a quiet stillness except for a few birds making their sounds in the distant trees.

The three dogs and I are climbing down the ledge to the garden. It is a small patch of color that has an abundance of plants and seeds peeping their heads above the damp cool earth.

As I look at each of my special friends, it would seem as though I can see smiles on each of their little dog faces. Duchess sits quietly nearby looking over the rest of us with a serene nobility of wisdom and honor bestowed upon the old. Then there comes Buddy, running chasing rabbits, eating flies and digging up who knows what. And Katie, what is she doing? Katie is sitting squarely on my lap. It is a bit awkward, as I feel I must pull some weeds, to compensate for this time of luxury and peacefulness.

At present we are in the strawberry patch which seems to require more attention than all the other plants. Katie has acquired a taste for strawberries. She is a bit wasteful, as she runs through the patch eating only half of every strawberry she sees.

Well the sun is slipping away down over the mountain range, so it is time to make our ascent up the hill once again to the house. Each of us feeling refreshed, and loved, and secure, knowing we belong to each other, as day melts into the stillness of night.

August 10, 1995

TIMMY COMES ON THE SCENE

I developed some treasured friends while living out in Shell. KL and Linda Reed lived just down the hill with their Pomeranian dogs. We became the dearest of friends and although I have lived here in Michigan for some time now, I miss them greatly

On the rare occasion I can drive out to Shell, it seems we hold onto every single word spoken. One of their little pets was named Big Mac. I suppose, although he was small in frame, he was a charmer.

Many neighborhood dogs looked just like Mac and we all knew why. Linda would bring her pets with her when she visited. We would be drinking coffee and sharing our latest novel we had read. In the meantime Big Mac would be entertaining Katie. It wasn't long before we were expecting puppies.

I had to be away across the state at a UW meeting so KL and Linda offered to keep Katie. I wanted the car to fly home. I was so anxious about the birth of the puppies. I made the lady driving her car stop at KL's before taking me home. The four little puppies had just been born about an hour earlier.

Oh, I was so disappointed I had missed out on all the excitement. KL said, "Well Patty, Katie is worn out, we need to keep her here tonight." My friends had been waiting for me, so I let them take me home, and in a few minutes I was back. I lovingly placed Katie and her babies in my car and we went home.

I gave three of the puppies to friends. Timmy was the smallest and it was apparent that he had a gentle spirit so I chose to keep him and am so thankful that I did.

Duchess had passed away and Buddy had been Shana's dog. She had married and moved to Seattle, so then the dog number was down to two.

KATIE DISAPPEARS

In the next few years, Thelma was faithful to her promise. Unfortunately one summer she was away on a trip when it was time for the county and state fair. Felix was a faithful family friend, so he volunteered to take Katie and Timmy up to his ranch on Clarks Fork River up north of Cody during the fairs.

I managed to get through a grueling work week at the county fair and now our staff would have to turn right around and head to state fair.

It was late Saturday night and I would be up again at 5:00 A.M. but I was so missing Katie and Timmy I just had to call Felix. The phone rang several times and then I heard a sleepy voice. "Hi Felix, I am sorry I know it is so late, but just wanted to know how Timmy and Katie are doing up at the ranch with you?" There was a long pause. "I hoped you wouldn't call." I knew this old friend so well.

I was so exhausted. I didn't want to hear what I knew he was going to have to tell me. "Katie is gone!" I managed to keep my voice at an even tone but it seemed all the oxygen went out of my lungs. "What happened, where did she go, how long has she been gone?"

"When I came home Thursday evening, Timmy was under the house howling and wouldn't come out and Katie wasn't with him." Katie and Timmy were inseparable; she never would have left him. Poor Felix, he would have to listen to the terrified howling of that little dog under the house for the next week as I would be working down at the state fair with the 4-H youth and would not be able to come to get Timmy until the next Sunday evening!

WYOMING 4-H FAMILY

My parents were always faithful 4-H leaders. My Dad was very involved in the sheep project. He and his close friend Lloyd Snider would travel to county fairs in the area and judge the sheep contests. Thursday was always the sheep contest day at Big Horn County fair.

I had sheep projects in 4-H and so many memories would come back of my father when I watched the young children with their sheep. I would work so hard all week, so I could watch some of the sheep judging contests on Thursday.

A contest to promote sewing with wool had been started years earlier by Lloyd's wife Bertie. It was called, "The Sheep Lead." The contestants who had made wool garments that year would model out in the arena escorting prize sheep. I was dedicated to promoting wool products, so I had been asked to participate with a designer garment I had made that year.

Every year at county fair I would find myself so sad on Thursday, knowing it was sheep contest day. The thoughts of my father would come, and keeping the tears back was sometimes just impossible. Early that morning I called my Mom. "Mom could you just drive over this afternoon and watch me in the Sheep Lead. I am just so sad today." Moms never stop being who they are, so sure enough, late that afternoon after I was all dressed waiting for the contest to begin I looked up into the stands, and there sat Mom and Felix.

I wiped away the tears, put a smile on my face and walked out there into the arena with a beautiful black faced Suffolk sheep following close behind.

Before Felix left his home, he put Katie and Timmy under the house with food and water. When he returned that evening, there was only one small dog and he was so traumatized, it would take a long time for Timmy to recover.

That week while I was at state fair, Melanie and her husband Larry walked up and down the river and all over the ranch looking for Katie, but she was never found. Katie was such a wonderful dog and she had been such a special mother to her puppies. My heart was so broken over her loss, but I also felt so badly for my friend Felix.

It was tormenting to me to think what could have happened to her. Coyotes are on the out skirts and eagles fly over head there near the cliffs. My rancher friends tried to console me, telling me if an eagle caught her she would die quickly, but that didn't seem to help much.

As I reflect on that time of losing my little dog Katie, I believe it did cause the bonding of Timmy and me.

When I finally could come home after a long workday and pick Timmy up he was still in a terrible state of mind.

He would cry and howl and shake. I would spend long hours just holding him and speaking softly to him. This went on for weeks and I was beginning to think, "What am I going to do with this little dog? Is he going to survive this tragedy, as I am sure he watched his mother die? After a few weeks of much tender loving care, Timmy and I settled into a peaceful state of being with each other. From that time on, Timmy became my shadow and with it a very tender relationship grew into a beautiful story of unconditional love on both sides from human and canine.

Timmy many times traveled with me through hill and dale. He was with me in the beginning of this life of writing. At times I felt badly, as he would patiently sit for hours under my feet as I worked so diligently on the research and writing of "Beloved Homeland." When he was much older and we had moved to Michigan he would be with me in the early morning hours as I prepared for the day of writing the shepherd book, "Reflections of a Wyoming Shepherd on the 23rd Psalm." He was a blessing in my life for eighteen long years.

The strange and mysterious thing about this emotion called grief is hopefully for most of us, it doesn't last forever. Life goes on. Life is different, but with the sorrow, we manage to put it in one of those rooms in the memory bank of life and then one day something happens when the door of that quiet room is opened.

This is what happened to me the other night when I called my dear and wonderful "Forever Friend," Mary Martin. Mary remembered how heartbroken I was over Katie, so she caused me to revisit that room of sorrow which had been closed away forever so long.

Timmy had passed away a few days earlier. I was relieved he was not suffering any more, but I felt such a sense of loss. Very early one morning, probably around 4:00 A.M. I was down by the garden watering Timmy's grave and the flowers. The sadness was so deep in my soul. That morning as I stood there in the silence of the forest thoughts began to form into sentences and stories of this journey with my loving pets. I knew my friend Mary would be so encouraging to me, so I called her late in the evening. Just as always she became my champion of encouragement.

She began to remind me of Katie. I was surprised that it was so fresh in her mind. "Patty, don't you remember that year at state fair, your heart was so sad. You knew something had happened to Katie and you were just broken hearted." When I got off the phone that night, I did go back into that room of memories of Katie.

I am so thankful for Mike and Thelma in their persistence in introducing me to that precious little puppy I named Katie. She was my treasured pet and wonderful mother to her puppies. She gave me Timmy and he will always be in my heart.

CHAPTER 4

IN THE GARDEN

Children have the concept that the day to day practices that are so common to families will always be the same. If I could go back to that time in my life, one thing for sure I would do is pay more attention to my mother's gardening skills. Those homestead wives were amazing women. The work load was heavy but they all managed to have huge gardens and canning was a big part of the summer activities. I spent many an afternoon out in the garden with my mother helping her with weeding, but for the most part I just prattled on like young children do. I started planting my own garden in those years in Shell, Wyoming. Summers were busy with all the 4-H activates and fairs, but coming home in the evening and spending time down in the garden with my pets, seemed to restore the calm of my spirit.

When I came to Michigan and bought my home, the back yard was a challenge. My neighbor told me of the older lady who had lived there for many years. I am sure she had passed away by the time this home was mine. That first spring I spent a lot of time digging up old stumps and getting rid of a lot of old foliage. Bit by bit I began to plant lovely flowering bushes. Each summer I would add several new garden plants and then one summer I made the wonderful little brick path that brought much more joy to my own heart then the grandchildren.

There was an old decorative cement bench the grandchildren would always pile on as if that was just their special place.

A memory that will always bring a smile to my face is when I think of those very early mornings when life was still quiet. I would go out with my cup of coffee, with Timmy at my side. I was always amused at how carefully he would step as the mornings were brisk and the grass was wet with dew. He would step ever so carefully sharing with me the joy of the garden and seeing what flowers were budding. When Timmy and I would return to the house, I would lovingly pick him up and dry off his feet and then we would go up to the office and begin our day of writing.

As we made our rounds of inspection, I would often quietly sing the old hymn, "In the Garden." Before I began to write today, I looked up the lyrics to this beautiful old song as the words so portray those thoughts of the closeness to God I would feel on those mornings. Mahalia Jackson's rendition of this old Hymn always goes to the deep place in my soul. I was almost sorry I had listened to her sing this old hymn this afternoon, for as I heard this beautiful woman's voice I wept as I just missed my mother so much.

IN THE GARDEN

I come to the garden alone
While the dew is still on the roses
And the voice I hear falling on my ear
The song of God discloses

And He walks with me
And He talks with me
And He tells me I am his own

And the joy we share as we tarry there
None other has ever known

He speaks and the sound of His voice
Is so sweet the birds hush their singing
And the melody that He gave to me
Within my heart is ringing

And He walks with me
And He talks with me
And He tells me I am his own
And the joy we share as we tarry there
None other has ever known

Charles Austin Miles (1868-1946)
Written in 1912

In this season of my life, I would say that writing is a beautiful gift. I am grateful for the strength and tenacity required to come to that quiet place sometimes days at a time to pen these stories of life that are so tender and many times filled with great emotion. By now, it is evident that my garden place has been a great source of creativity for me for many years. I will share with you some of those snippets of stories relating to my garden and flowers and maple trees, many times as I was recovering from my car wreck or before and after surgeries, nature would be my muse as I would feel the nearness of God.

Growing up on the northern plains of Wyoming we did not have the luxury of the rich foliage and trees that describe Michigan, so the beautiful scenery always brings me pleasure. I will always have a special place in my heart for Wyoming, as that is my old stomping ground. There are many parts of Wyoming that are void of trees and one could almost classify the terrain as barren, but then it does have those massive Rocky Mountains that are the great love of the McClaflin family. When my parents came to their new homestead in 1950 to farm on virgin soil, there were no trees for miles. All of the families worked diligently planting trees, but very few survived. Coming from that rough terrain of survival, I have a great love and respect for trees.

I had loved my old vintage home so well and knew what I would miss the most was my backyard garden and the sunroom. Although it was December when this apartment became my new home, I asked the office staff if I could live back by the forest and they graciously honored my request.

How quickly we can forget those details of life that might seem small, but in reality they are very important

This morning early, as those thoughts of writing were coming to mind, I looked at my computer screen and saw the icon for the picture of the tallest tree in the forest. Well maybe it wasn't, but from my view from the deck it did appear to be the tallest.

When Springport Glenn became my new home the forest out in front of my deck was filled with trees and bushes void of leaves. I knew stories would evolve from the tree out in front which appeared to me to be the tallest tree in the forest. I actually awaited the arrival of spring. To my great dismay my tallest tree had no leaves that spring. I would go out and examine the huge trunk and look up into the sky to the tallest branches, and sure enough I do believe the tree was dead. One morning I heard the loud sawing and looked out with great sadness to see they were cutting down this magnificent tree.

By the end of the day, that massive mighty tree had been cut down. I would walk over with Timmy and inspect the trunk, feeling a great sadness of stories that would not be written. The tree took up a good deal of space, so in a short time, large bushes and tall weeds filled in the space. I asked the office staff if I could plant a flower garden and maybe have some benches to sit on. They thought it was a great idea, but with the busyness of life, the summer came to a close and winter sat in. In the early spring I was approached again to see if I still wanted to have a project, but by then the surgery was scheduled so that was the end of my planning and dreaming of a beautiful garden space.

In those last few years when I still lived in my home I was very aware Timmy was getting old and I knew one day I would have to bury him, so I would look out in the back of the garden for that very right place for this little pet. Life does have its turns and surprises and now I find myself in an apartment looking out over a forest of trees. I had so loved my old vintage home, but have come to the understanding it was far more then I was able to manage in this season of my own life.

When friends ask me how I like apartment living, I come back with a smile on my face. "I am so happy, that I am so happy."

I will have to say that very quickly this cozy little apartment became a very peaceful and contented home for Timmy and me.

Very early this spring I had to undergo some major surgery from complications from the car wreck in Wyoming. I thought I would be back to work in a week. I just laugh now. No, it was a six weeks stint and even then I really wasn't up to it, but went back any way. In those first few weeks I would take short walks with Timmy but couldn't move my arms. I knew his little heart was giving him trouble so we wouldn't go very far, as I was not able to pick him up. It was the end of winter, so there were no leaves on the trees yet. As we walked down the dirt path, I would look over to my left and daydream about a small hidden place where I could plant a few tomatoes. After a few weeks I came to the conclusion that was not even logical. It was a Friday morning in early June my three friends, Mary Ellen, Carol and Patsy came to see me. They had waited some time to make sure I was up to the visit. They had forbidden me to make the lemon meringue pie, but I did anyway, as they knew I would. As they walked into my apartment that morning, I saw a tall handsome man standing behind them. I didn't know who he was. He came right in with the women.

I had left my garden and flowers behind at my beloved home, but now the 9' x 7' deck would have to suffice. With my creative artist mind and soul, a great deal of planning went into this small garden plot. For looking out on the forest of trees are multi-colored flower pots with an array of color from light pink, lemon yellow to deep purple.

On the right wall I am growing tomatoes, onions, herbs, onions and green peppers. The blinds on the glass sliding door are for the most part open all the time.

I even brought home an American flag for the fourth of July. It took two hours to tape, wire and use every other thing I had available to get it to stand out on the lawn. The neighbor fellow down stairs later said, "Why didn't you ask me to help you." I thought, "Where were you when I needed you." Anyway, it is all wonderful and I feel greatly blessed.

Now back to the gentlemen walking out to my deck. "My name is Todd, I like to garden; can I look at your flowers." I told him I was so happy in my apartment, but I so missed my garden in the home I had owned, as that was my muse as a writer.

Since I have lived here, I have thought so many times how nice it would be if I could just look out over at the forest edge and have a small garden. Todd said, "How would you like a garden out there." Well that is just what I had thought myself.

After Todd left, my friends were elated for me. While we were eating our warm lemon meringue pie, we talked of how uncanny, for that man to walk in just as they arrived and that made it all the more special.

That was Friday. On Sunday afternoon I made my way out to the football field at Napoleon High school to watch my twin granddaughters, Anna and Elizabeth in their high school graduation. It was up in the high eighties that afternoon as we celebrated together as a family.

I drove home after five and there was Todd out there in all those weeds and rocks and tree stumps with a roto tiller. He looked exhausted as he had been working for hours. There are not words to express how full of joy I was that evening.

The area was covered with poison ivy so he had to spray. I had to wait two weeks to plant and I wondered if anything would be harvested that year.

The first day I carried all my seeds, shovels and water can out to the garden plot, Marvin my neighbor in the lower apartment came out and asked if he could help. We worked on and on, as it was not an easy undertaking. There were many large slat rocks that he lifted out of the ground that would later become the path through the garden. I was so grateful for his help, as I was still recovering from surgery, and the task before me was really more than I could handle.

We both worked hard out in the garden that summer. Todd rigged up some worn out hoses, which leaked, but I got into my stash and we taped and taped. It would take both Marvin and me to pull the hoses across the parking lot. Mr. Ground hog ate the green bean plants several times, but we did have squash and the tomatoes that first summer.

As I look back over that summer, I am becoming more aware that the grieving process for this little pet was already happening. I knew he was failing fast, and by the last few weeks I didn't even want to spend too much time out in the garden. I talked to Marvin about my pet and we discussed a good place to bury him. I thought maybe right up next to the tree near the garden as the ground wouldn't be trampled.

For those of us who love our pets, there is an understanding that we share. One of those defining realities for each of us is that we are almost ashamed at how much we love that dog or cat or bird or whatever. Another defining factor is that the life expectancy for pets is far shorter than for most of us.

At least we hope that is the situation, for we have heard of the dedicated dog who sits on the grave of his master and somehow that seems more tragic.

It was a hot afternoon when my family came and the mosquitoes were thick when we buried Timmy. Paul could not dig near the tree as the roots were so heavy, so he came out a ways. He couldn't dig very deep, so I was very concerned over the grave, so he pulled over some of the heaviest slate rock and covered over where Timmy was buried. I knew Shana was watching me carefully, but there were no tears that afternoon. I was just numb.

As I reflect back over the many years of loving pets and sharing my garden experiences with them, I believe it brings a smile on the face of our Shepherd of Heaven, as the world and all of its beauty was his plan for his children. I learned long ago that God commands a hand in the entire universe and yet he cares about the smallest details of mankind. Timmy was my loving little buddy for ever so long. I wanted his memory to be close to me, so I am blessed that he lived long enough to come to this new dwelling place and now I can go down to the garden early in the morning and water the flowers next to his grave. The grief that was so heavy at first has now turned into a grateful heart for all the cherished memories I will carry with me.

SECTION II

AND THEN THERE IS GRIEF AND HOW TO SURVIVE IT

CHAPTER 5

FIVE STAGES OF GRIEF

This portion will be brief but can be a very important tool in navigating through times of grief. Depending on the circumstances surrounding grief it is possible to be able to go directly to acceptance and life can move on without much interruption.

I think for myself personally, I went through all five stages of grief with my father's death. I remember feeling overwhelmed at times, as I had never experienced such sorrow. There is no set pattern in dealing with grief, and at times in the process a person might find themselves going back and reliving a stage.

What is vital for those who surround the grieving individual is to have an empathic ear and heart in allowing the time it takes, as it is not a wasted time in life. "There are responses to loss that many people have, but there is not a typical response to loss, as there is no typical loss. Our grief is as individual as our lives." *Kubler-Ross, page 7

When I visited my mother several years ago she said she couldn't remember what Daddy looked like. So of course, when I went home I pulled out the family pictures and made copies of Daddy and sent them to her. I miss him greatly, but I came to peace and acceptance many years ago.

My brother Wayne describes it perfectly as Daddy has been gone over thirty years and that is a very long time. Wayne said, "It seems like thirty years, and sometimes it seems like yesterday."

I have listed several books at the end of the chapter if you the reader are struggling in trying to navigate through your own grief process.

DENIAL

I describe the first stage of grief one might expect in denial, as a protective layer over the heart and mind. One scripture that comes in view as I am writing is Psalm 139:14.

I will praise You, for I am fearfully and wonderfully made;
Marvelous are Your works, And that my soul knows very well.

These words are often described as the physical part of mankind, but as I look back over my own journey I have come to realize that the way the Creator thinks of the mind is amazing. In those times of grief if one has learned to trust this Shepherd of Heaven, it becomes very apparent that he truly cares about all those details of our lives. This is especially cherished when our heart is broken in the times of denial when we are trying to wrap our minds around the reality of it all. "When we are in denial, we may respond at first by being paralyzed with shock or blanketed with numbness.' The denial is still not denial of the actual death, even though someone may be saying, "I can't believe he's dead." The person is actually saying that, at first, because it is too much for his or her psyche."

*Kubler-Ross page 8

One of saddest examples of prolonging the stage of denial was the mother who had lost her teen-age daughter. Each evening as the other children and father came to the dinner table, there was a place set for the daughter who would never return. The mother did not live long enough to see grandchildren, so what a loss for the rest of the family.

"Living our lives in denial may not be very exciting, but it helps us feel safe. At least that is what we tell ourselves. But in settling for an imagined sense of security and safety, we lose our capacity to take risks and experience life as the adventure it was meant to be." *Westfall, page 168

When one is walking through the stage of denial, it can be a coping mechanism to give time for the reality of the circumstance or tragedy to become manageable. One of the aspects that can come out of these times of grief, is developing the capacity and kindness as we see others in their own grief; giving them encouragement and hope that they will survive the heartache of it all.

ANGER

I remember the day I was going to write the portion on the step in grief called "Anger." Oh I could circle around a lot of topics and stash this one at the bottom of the pile.

You might ask, "why are you someone who struggles with anger?' Well not exactly: I grew up thinking I was not allowed to be angry. I am sure you have met someone like me. You know, there is a name for us. Let me see: here are just a few definitions; peacemaker, gracious, problem solver, compliant child, easy going, passive, naïve; I think that should give a semblance of where we are going with this.

TAME THAT TIGER

Just as in times past in writing, I have found myself going back and relying on many life experiences in telling the story. I am most grateful for the many encouragers and educators who have invested in me and given me tools to enrich my life.

As I wrote this portion I thought of those many "Forever Friends" who have played such key roles in this journey of life.

Soon after coming back to Wyoming and taking a position with UW Cooperative Extension, Ben Silliman, Family Life Specialist came on the scene. He introduced me to a wide scope of Family Resiliency research that would become an intricate part of all the work and educational programs I would conduct in the future.

Another key player, who had been a close neighbor and friend from childhood, was Teddy Jones. She also worked with UW Extension as a 4-H Educator in the adjacent county which happened to be Park County, where I had grown up. Teddy and I volunteered to teach programs on Anger Management in the Big Horn Basin area. We had varied audiences from many walks of life, so as time progressed, we fashioned the programs to meet the needs of class participants.

After a while we came up with a title which seemed to fit the work shop topics. It was not original with our programs, as it has been used many times in a variety of advertisements down through the years. "Tame That Tiger," seemed to carry the message we were conveying of this emotion called anger and how to manage it in productive and healing ways.

Early on in our work, we volunteered to teach a three-part series to a local group of teen-agers from a group home for troubled teens. We planned and organized well, as we divided up the portions we would teach. After the first session, I remember we were walking out to our cars and I do believe both of us were exhausted from the morning of teaching. Teddy had worked with young people for years, and she had a gift for caring and understanding.

She turned to me and asked, "Patty who are these young people and where have they come from?" I looked at her and reminded her that I had told her about this group home for troubled youth. Well I don't know if that information had just past over or I hadn't made it clear to her. At least for the next two sessions we had some idea of pulling out all those creative ways of reaching troubled children.

What remains with me to this day about that three session work shop on "Anger Management,' was the last day after we had concluded the work shop. We gave the young people evaluations to fill out, which we knew would be a challenge. We asked if there was anything anyone wanted to share. One young man around sixteen years of age raised his hand. I had observed him throughout the sessions, recognizing many times he appeared to be agitated and uncomfortable. Teddy and I were amazed at what he had to say. "I just want to thank you for coming to teach us. You have taught me so much and given me so many tools, I think now I can manage my anger and be able to have a good life." Wow! To hear that brought joy to our hearts.

Often I would find myself, regardless of the group, telling them how I wish I could have had a class like this when I was growing up. Another point I would make, and I was careful to try and not offend anyone in the audience, is that in relation to my own life, one of those attributes I have been the most grateful for was when life happened that was difficult and I found myself unable to forgive myself or others, as I prayed, God always answered my prayer and allowed me to lean into his forgiving power. This would in turn help me to cope with anger if it was a part of the situation.

DEATH OF A PARENT

From the time we are young, we recognize that one day we will say good bye for the last time to our parents. Sometimes death comes quickly, without the opportunity to say those last words. In some situations, our parent leaves us, but they are still living, such as in the case with Alzheimer's. This is especially a brutal experience for the family living out this loved ones sickness. No matter how we prepare for the death of a parent it is just hard. For some they pass through this phase and don't experience the stages of death described by <u>Elisabeth Kubler-Ross</u> in her extensive research of death and grieving.

This was not going to be the case for me when it came to my father's death. Looking back on that time, I do believe I experienced all five stages of grief. I can also say that I grew in character and the beauty of living because of that process I walked through.

By now I am sure you the reader, have come to realize, he was a very significant person in my life. He passed away in late July. Fall came and the teaching year with all the other many tasks of life continued on in a normal pattern, except I was not the same. It seemed I walked around in a daze, just going through the motions of living.

It had been almost a year to the day after the death of my father. For some reason on that afternoon, the children must have been off to youth camp and the house was silent.

I went out in the sunroom, closed all the windows and the crying started. It was that kind of cry you don't want anyone to hear. There were times on a Sunday morning, when the hymns were sung, I couldn't hold back the tears but the crying was silent for the most part. Looking back on that time, I seemed to have a sense the whole congregation grieved for me.

The tears on this afternoon were not quiet; they were like a raging flood. After about an hour, I was totally exhausted. I began to speak out loud to God and the words I spoke frightened me. "God I am so angry with you. I prayed so hard for my Dad to be healed. You know what is going on in my life. How will I ever be able to let him go?"

I don't know that I had ever before in my life told God I was mad at him. Just saying those words was frightening to me. What happened next has changed my life. The love I had always had for God grew with such a dimension and with it the ability to come to an acceptance of the death of my father. The room became completely silent and it seemed as if the love of my Heavenly Father filled the whole room with peace to my broken heart. As a girl growing up caring for bum lambs, it was easy for me to understand the scriptures dealing with the Shepherd speaking to his sheep.

My sheep hear My voice, and I know them, and they follow Me. And I give them eternal life, and they shall never perish; neither shall anyone snatch them out of My hand.
John 10:27-28 NKJV

This was not an audible voice, it was silent. But the words silently spoken were profound to this heartbroken follower so bewildered in grief. "You cannot comprehend now what has happened to you, but I understand your sorrow and I am very acquainted with grief. I have been so close to you in these months when you have felt such despair. Give me your anger and I will carry your burden for you. In this time of such pain, I have enlarged your heart. This is a painful process, but from this day forward you will never be the same.

You will be able to take on a greater degree of compassion and love for the broken hearted. Your father is safe and well and he will always be in your heart until I bring you home to be with me."

Down through the years, although my father is in Heaven he is so close in my memories. In this book about grief and in all of my writings you will see his gentle presence in my life.

That bitter cold night out in Shirley Basin when I was so cold and so near death, it was as if he was sitting there right next to me, saying. "Don't' give Patty, you have so much to accomplish." So here I am today, with the picture my sister Linda, so lovingly took of my father and me sharing moments in time just a month before he went home. I miss him greatly, but I am not sad now. I just want to be present for my own children and grandchildren.

As one walks through grief, depending on the circumstances and how they impact one's life, I would have to say walking through that time of my father's death brought me into a place of beauty in life.

This scripture took on a new meaning for me with the death of my father as I came to understand more fully how God cares about the smallest of details.

For this we say to you by the word of the Lord, that we who are alive and remain until the coming of the Lord will by no means precede those who are asleep. For the Lord Himself will descend from heaven with a shout, with the voice of an archangel and with the trumpet of God. And the dead in Christ will rise first. Then we who are alive and remain shall be caught up together with them in the clouds to meet the Lord in the air. And thus we shall always be with the Lord. Therefore comfort one another with these words.

I Thessalonians 4:13 – 18 NKJV

The stage of anger which was always hard for me to accept was not such a barrier to living after that. Anger is a normal emotion in life. For some, it is not a problem, as they can carry a great deal of anger and pass it all around. But for those of us who seem to have taken on the misconception that anger is not allowed; well that is not healthy and many times we find ourselves in the place of carrying the burden of someone else's anger. Not allowing ourselves to just be honest and admit in this time of sorrow, we are angry only makes the time of grief extend farther into our lives. To stuff down our emotions and not be truthful with ourselves, can create a host of other heartaches. As I am writing this morning I am thinking about our Shepherd of Heaven, knowing he has experienced all the emotions you and I will face in this life. He can handle your anger. In fact, he longs to come along side of you and help you put those pieces of your emotions, so raw, back together, and then you can go on in your personal journey.

Be strong and of good courage, do not fear nor be afraid of them;
for the Lord your God,
He is the One who goes with you.
He will not leave you nor forsake you.
Deuteronomy 31:6 NJKV

BARGAINING

The journey through grief is a very personal time. Depending on the circumstances that have caused the grief the impact for individuals cannot always fall into categories or even stages.

The human mind takes comfort in putting life into boxes or stages that flow on a linear line.

At times this will work but what does one do when the grief seems to consume the oxygen in the room and life can never be the same again.

Research conducted by Alan Wolfelt indicates this is not always the case. His compassionate approach to grief has been well documented in his book, "Understanding Your Grief, Ten Essential Touchstones for Finding Hope and Healing Your Heart." If you find yourself in the stage of bargaining, asking yourself, "What if," and there are no answers, just be patient with yourself.

As others observe a loved one or friend walking through personal grief, it takes a great deal of compassion and patients to allow them to walk this journey. If they themselves have never experienced grief, self-discipline will be required to not try and hurry the process along.

"Bargaining can help our mind move from one state of loss to another. It can be a way station that gives our psyche the time it may need to adjust. Bargaining may fill the gaps that our strong emotions generally dominate, which often keep suffering at a distance. It allows us to believe that we can restore order to the chaos that has taken over. Bargaining changes over time. We may start our bargaining for our loved one to be saved. Later, we may even bargain that we might die instead of our loved one." *Kubler-Ross, page 19

It is easy for the on-looker in this state of grief you are going through to comment, "Time Heals all Wounds." If you are in the bargaining stage, this only aids in bringing on despair and depression. Hopefully there is someone in your life, who has walked through this process themselves and they can just quietly come along side and walk down this path with you.

If you feel isolated and alone at this time, put this memory in your back pocket, for very likely after this season of sorrow passes, there will be someone you will be able to walk alongside who also has no one, and somehow this will give you your own personal strength to head into the wind.

DEPRESSION

This morning as I write I can look over to the side and see the picture I took of my mother a while back when I visited her in Wyoming. The eyes that had been so bright and full of life are now dim but the tender loving smile is saying, "Keep going daughter, you are so close to the finish line now".

After those few days with her, sitting there reading her stories out of my books, I was weary and the sadness came. More than the sadness, was a resiliency of spirit, knowing I had walked through deep waters of depression in the past, and come up higher on the mountain of compassion and understanding. It became apparent as I recognized those feelings of sorrow early in the morning walking through my little garden; I once again was reliving what I had been writing the in last few months.

When the sadness and depression settles over life everything seems to move in slow motion. While walking through this journey of grief, we wonder if we will ever overcome. Will life ever be normal again? Well, for sure, life will not be as we have known it in the past. "After bargaining, our attention moves squarely into the present. Empty feelings present themselves, and grief enters our lives on a deeper level, deeper than we ever imagined. This depressive stage feels as though it will last forever.

It's important to understand that this depression is not a sign of mental illness. It is the appropriate response to a great loss." *Kubler-Ross, page 20

    I once had a writing instructor tell me, "Write down your thoughts and feelings during this time of sorrow, as soon they will be locked away from your memory." Even if you do not consider yourself a writer, during this stage, I recommend writing in a personal journal, as there is great value in writing down those thoughts, as somehow it makes life more manageable.

    My first writing was in the form of poems written in a writing journal, now yellow with age. It is my personal journey that is not shared with others. I rarely read those poems, but when I do, I am struck with the depth of feelings I was brave enough to pen to the page.

    During that first season of writing, my world seemed to have turned upside down, as life surely was never going to be the same again. I came to understand, even though the sadness seemed to take the breath out of me, if I could just manage to get to the keyboard the words would come.

Oh, there were times the weeping was relentless. I call those years I lived in Shell, Wyoming as, "The back side of the desert," or one might call them the "Arabia years".

I came to understand during that stage of grief that God wastes nothing in our lives, if we will just reach up to him and allow him to soothe our wounded heart. This is one of those poems I wrote in the beginning months of writing. Upon occasion I bring it out once again and share with another who seems overwhelmed in their own personal sadness.

ROBES OF COMFORT

Father I am sitting at your feet today. I am moving as close as I can.
Your robes of love surround me, I am so thankful for that.
Can't seem to keep the tears back, as they stream down my face.
I wipe them away with the hem, weaved into the body of your cloak.
As you know, I have occupied this place so many times from the time I was a small child.
I have so wanted to be like you, have your heart of compassion.
I am questioning myself today, this love I feel so deep.
The cost is very high. It leaves me so vulnerable, easily taken advantage of.
Could opt for bitterness and vengeance, somehow I know I must fight that choice.
As I look up to you, I see the love in your eyes.
I so long for that solace,
I want to see others through your vision.
I find myself longing for that same love to spend on others.
I must keep walking with you.

I will stand soon, but right now, I am setting very close to you Father. Just let me catch my breath, then I will continue on my journey.

January 13, 1995, Patricia Booher

ACCEPTANCE

In this journey of life, if we take the time to look around, we will see others walking through their own grief process. Regardless of the circumstances that surround grief, it is just not a fun time of life

If I told you, the reader, this portion inserted on the stages of grief have been easy to pen, well that would not be telling you the truth. For as I write to you, my mind does go back to times in my own journey, when I wondered would I have joy again, would I ever be able to really just laugh that deep and robust sound my family loves to hear. I have an artist's eye for beauty in nature and maybe if in my own journey I had not experienced deep sorrow, I would just walk by this beautiful display of exposed roots from the lemon balm plant. I have referred back so many times to this scripture when stages of grief racked my heart and soul and the words always gave me courage.

If you look at the date "Maple Leaves" was written, you will understand I was still living in my old vintage home with the garden that Timmy and I would stroll through every morning before a day of writing. I have included this snippet of a story as I believe it so expresses this final stage of acceptance in walking through grief.

As you read down through this collection of thoughts regarding the lemon balm plant, read between the lines and know you too one day will see more clearly and be able to relate to others who are sorrowing. Life once again will become beautiful for you as well.

"For I know the plans I have for you," declares the Lord, "plans to prosper you and not to harm you, plans to give you hope and a future. "Then you will call on me and come and pray to me, and I will listen to you. You will seek me and find me when you seek me with all your heart.
Jeremiah 29:11-13

MAPLE LEAVES, LEMON BALM AND EXPOSED ROOTS

    For those of us who are poets, writers and artist, the world is seen through a different lens. If life has taught us wisdom, we have grown accustomed to this prism of color and emotion.

Realizing not everyone walks this same path and we come to a place of respect for that other fellow traveler on his or her own journey.

These last few days, my love of nature has called to me as the early sun rises. I reach over and pull open the curtains as the dawn hits the new leaves folding out into a fan on the maple tree next to the deck. As I walk out into the dew encrusted grass with my little Yorky, we inspect each new mound of tulip bulbs as they begin their announcement of spring.

The deep purple violets were the last to lay open folds of rich contrast to the soft feather like petals of pink chiffon.

I live on a limited income these days, so it took a lot of gumption last fall for me to just decide to do it. I went to the store and picked out two big bags of tulip bulbs. I had heard about the squirrels stealing the bulbs out of the ground so I thought a great deal about how to outwit them. I went to the local hardware store and found the little grandpa type and told him of my plan. He set me up with a heavy metal mesh screen and metal cutters.

As I began to cut out the pieces of mesh, I had to use heavy leather gloves, so I wouldn't cut my hands. I prayed that I wouldn't get a cold, as it was late October and my lungs are a challenge. The anticipation of the spring bulbs coming up gave me stamina to complete my task. I planted mounds of bulbs at focal points around the yard and covered them with the mesh and dried maple leaves. Then I laid heavy bricks on the mesh and added some of my collection of rocks from Lake Michigan. The rains came and snow soon followed.

In the early spring I checked daily, not wanting to remove my arsenal of protection too early. My Yorky and I watched daily for squirrels and a few times we weren't fast enough. I actually began to pray for those little bulbs in the ground. By this time, you have come to realize that these little flowers out in my garden beds are a very big deal to me.

And for that reason, I am surprised that another plant next to my wooden steps leading from my deck has become such a daily focal point for me. The leaves are just beginning to take form on the branches.

A few unwanted maple seedlings have popped up, along with some volunteer lemon balm leaves which make a citron green frame encircling this flowering bush.

What drew me down to the ground for a closer inspection were the exposed roots wrapped around each other, almost giving one the thoughts of self-preservation. As the cool morning rays of sun slipped through the maple canopy overhead, I zoomed in on the roots with my camera. After making a copy of my picture, I sat down on the step and pulled a few lemon balm leaves; enjoying the aroma, as I studied the intricate weaving of roots imbedded in rich garden soil.

Very soon I will take my small garden spade and ever so carefully cover the roots for protection from insects and other of nature's elements. But for now I am drawn to this picture of life, knowing the winter rains and snow have washed away the protection of dark heavy earth.

Nature has such a beautiful way of speaking to the soulish part of man, if he will only allow himself the blessing of quiet. On this silent afternoon, as I study once more the small picture pasted above my computer screen, my emotions are drawn down into that place where my own roots of spirit are exposed. Such courage one takes in sharing those places of the heart that have been buried deep, sometimes never again to come to the surface.

It is the mature traveler who recognizes when to keep roots covered from view. But then there are times in our journey we come across another who has not made it as far in recovery and acceptance. And for that one, we will let those roots be uncovered once again in order to bring courage to the broken hearted.

"This time will pass, the pain will never completely go away, but you will learn to manage it. You will also come to a time that this sorrow has actually made your life richer, as you realize how very precious this gift of life is. Friends will become more precious. Family roots will grow deeper. And the awareness that the Shepherd of Heaven is ever so close, bringing a healing balm like no other fragrance allows one a deeper realization of just how much he loves and cares for his own."

Patricia Booher May 4, 2010

Kubler-Ross, Elisabeth and David Kessler, <u>On Grief and Grieving</u>. Scribner, New York. 1992.
Pages 7, 8, and 20.
Westfall, John F., <u>Getting Past What You'll Never Get Over</u>. Page 168, Revell, Grand Rapids. Michigan. Page 168
Wolfelt, Alan D. PhD, <u>Understanding Your Grief</u>. Companion Press, Fort Collins, Colorado. 2003.

CHAPTER 6
THANKFULNESS

As you the reader may recognize, so often, when I begin writing on a new topic a song from my past seems to come to the surface, I believe the words of the melody are appropriate now for I am speaking of the tool of "Thankfulness."

If you are in the beginning stages of grief, this might be more than you can comprehend, but I encourage you to take note of those everyday happenings that make the sorrow more manageable for you. It might seem less painful to not take the time to be quiet, but grief takes a toll. Regardless the reason for the grief, if one can take a reprieve and allow God's spirit to bring comfort, then the climb up the mountain of survival becomes possible. When we look back, faith can grow as we can be thankful for how far we have come.

"Be Still and Know that I am God."

Be still and know that I am God,
Be still and know that I am God,
Be still and know that I am God,
I am the Lord that healeth thee,
I am the Lord that healeth thee,
I am the Lord that healeth thee,
In thee, O Lord, I put my trust,
In thee, O Lord, I put my trust,
In thee, O Lord, I put my trust,

Melody of unknown origin, harmony by Stephen Dean.
Music arrangement@1999Stephen Dean.

The other day I drove back to the apartment where I had planted a garden out in the forest. It will be a relief when this book is in print as the next novel will be filled with many happy stories of life during those years out in my garden patch. (<u>Lessons of Life I Learned in my Garden Patch</u>.) I have vowed that will be the last time I go there as the garden has revolved back into forest. The beautiful English garden Timmy and I had spent so many hours developing is now full of old leaves, branches, and trash. I went over to where I had buried Timmy and saw the rock I hand painted the words on, "Timmy's Grave." I am surprised the rock is still there, but I have brought it home with me. I am not sad now over my little Yorky I had loved for so many years, but am thankful for the memories. They have been stored now in the snippets of stories that hopefully will bring comfort to another who is going through their own journey of grief.

Those years when I worked at Sam's as one of those demonstration representatives for a multitude of products, I learned many aspects of life of which I hope I never forget. For the most part, those filing by my table for a sample were courteous and respectful and then there were the others we won't discuss. Looking back on those times when life was hard and I was going through grief, because of my work ethic I just kept doing the job before me. I would be so thankful for that one who came along to lift me. I have resolved for the rest of my life journey, no matter who waits on me, I will tell them as I leave the check-out stand, "Have a Blessed Day." That is a very small gesture, but maybe that is the only kind word that person who has value received that day.

The days before holidays were beyond stressful and it seems looking back on it now, Mother's Day brought with it many layers of emotions.

Several years ago while working I watched as customers filed by, many with stress written across their faces. One lady said, "After my mother died, I just told my children, I don't want to celebrate mother's day anymore." This emotion called grief can tear out our hearts. Sad for her children, as I am sure they surely love their mother and want to honor her on this special day.

In this last year as we have walked through the ravages of Covid, my heart is saddened when I think of those mothers who have passed away and many were not able to say Good-By to loved ones.

This last weekend was Mother's Day and I have to confess, I am grateful I am slowly recovering from my own bout with Covid. I am thankful I was able to spend the day with family. What topped off the evening was watching my great-granddaughter celebrate her 3rd birthday. As Claire tore through the packages, when she came to Anna's gift all others faded away as it was a horse. Seems like she takes after grandma as at that age I also was a lover of horses.

I recognize that sorrow can be acquainted with that day of the year we call "Mother's Day." I have read some social media this year suggesting we should just forget this day as there are those who are sad. I would not recommend this as a way of coping.

White Wool, Beads and Silk Ribbon Flowers

Several years ago my mother was moving to her new dwelling in a nursing home near where I had lived in Shell, Wyoming. I longed to go be with her so flew out for a few days. Looking back on that time, each moment with her is etched in my thoughts of cherished memories now. I will describe in more detail about my mother's dress in the book on "Creativity," that will be written soon. I suppose it is because I am a dress designer that I had been fretting about what we would bury her in when she passed away. My heart was heavy as I left her that last morning. On the plane trip home I began to create in my mind, "Why don' I make my mom a dress." The dress turned into a work of art for me as I would bead, make silk flowers, and design the pattern. I would call it a process of grieving for her as she was now so very old.

When I showed my son Craig the dress, he saw the intricate work that had gone into the making of it. He ask, "Mom how long did this take you?" I replied, "Oh a while," knowing it had been many months. When I gave her the dress, she knew it was my way of saying, "Mom if I searched the world over, it would be you I would choose to be my Mom."

As I think about that day with my Mom, I am so grateful I was able to give her the dress in person. It is a precious memory to me now.

I will stop with that sentence or there will be no more writing today.

I will reflect back to myself, so I can give you a space of safety if you just might be that one who doesn't know how you will ever get through this grief. It is not important that I give you the specifics, but I have to say there have been life situations that so shattered my heart and soul, I really didn't know if I would be whole again. I did not realize before my own grief that it was possible for a human being to feel such sorrow and despair.

At this time it is very likely you are not able to say you are thankful for your sorrow. The last thing you need is to have the negative judgment cast over you, as it only causes the pain to drive deeper into your soul.

I came to the conclusion long ago, I just don't have some answers in this life and maybe one day when I am in Heaven I won't need an answer.

To be honest with you the reader, I don't know in this life if I would ever be able to say to a person in tragedy to just be thankful for the situation. As I look back on my own life, there have been those heart aches that can resurface, but as time has passed and I am in a place of emotional safety where I can reflect, I can say I am thankful and so grateful that I have now understood that the Lord never left me alone for a moment. I do believe I have some semblance of the words in Isaiah 53 that speaks of Jesus Christ, being a man of sorrows and acquainted with grief.

He is despised and rejected by men,
A Man of sorrows and acquainted with grief.
Isaiah 53:3 NKJV

As I have observed others and as well myself with my own life experiences, I have come to realize that the ability to be thankful goes a long way in coping with grief. This simple but profound ability to be thankful can make the difference of despair verses integrity in overcoming any situation.

I have to admit there have been times in which I found I did not have the capacity to be thankful or even forgive in my own strength. It was in those times, in my soul and spirit, I would see myself at the foot of the cross, and recognizing what Jesus suffered so I could be free when the weeping of the night would be over and peace could come to my troubled heart.

You might be that one who lives in an environment of negativity and criticism. This has been the model you have been given. To break out of that mold requires a great deal of courage and determination. I refer back to the words of the song at the beginning of this chapter. In the next few chapters I will share some snippets of my own journey. You can read between the lines, as there were some situations that required more that I was able to handle in myself and in those times I had to go to that silent place with God, but as you read when I came into the stage of acceptance, then I was able to go to another and hopefully bring comfort.

During this winter when I was so gravely ill with Covid, I describe it as the silent days; I had such a sense of destiny. I have learned from past experiences that built a resolve which built courage and faith I would survive. I will come back to this tool of being thankful. Each morning I would come in to the living room, open the blinds and crawl under heavy quilts and just tell the Lord I was thankful as I knew this situation could be so much worse.

I was so grateful that now I was in this peaceful cottage that looked out on the frozen lake of Michigan and that would bring peace to my soul.

I have referred to my own grief in this small book. But much more than sadness, as I look back and reflect of those difficult times and see the many kindness shown to me, my heart is full of thankfulness.

I would not classify these snippets of stories of my own life I have shared to be profound. I trust as you read on you will see the thread of being able to recognize those tiny things through the day that would give me a spark of hope and comfort, even in the most trying of circumstances. I do believe that as we humble ourselves and pray we will appreciate the tiny and sometimes minuscule blessings in life, then when the big stuff happens, we will be able to face it.

WHEN THE LITTLE THINGS BECOME THE BIG STUFF OF LIFE

One morning when I still lived in the apartment I was writing snippets of stories and began to remember the old dented coffee percolator my parents had used for years. In the early mornings, my dad would get up and fix a pot of coffee. I remember him sitting there in his old recliner chair as he would watch the sun come up in the eastern sky. And then the thoughts would come, when after a busy work day, I would drive out and visit with my mom over a cup of coffee, long after my dad had passed away.

Later in the afternoon I went out to my son Craig's home to help my grandson trim the branches in the rose garden.

After we had completed our garden project, we came into the house. I was telling my daughter-in-law, Sandy that I had been thinking about that old percolator of my parents. I just wished I had somehow kept it around, as it had so many precious memories for me. She said, "Oh I have something for you." She went to her closet and pulled out a little case. When she opened it up, I felt such a nostalgic joy. She said she had found it one day at a garage sale and thought it might be used some time for a camping trip. I told her she needed to keep it, but I would like to borrow it for a time and would return it later.

I have to say I am one of those who truly loves those tiny and simple things of life and for that I believe my life is rich. I brought the little kit home and sat the coffee pot right on the edge of the counter.

I also collect china cups and mugs and each morning I make a choice of just the right color for the day's activities.

Now, I don't need one more cup in my cupboard, but one day I saw this happy little mug in a dollar store. The coral color, with the chartreuse green rim brings a smile to my face. It is not necessarily a pretty cup but it does give me a sense of those farm days of ever so long ago now.

I took a picture of my happy yellow coffee pot with the cup setting next to it, to give you a semblance of how very small it is. Yes, I would have to say it is those little things in life; those times of drinking coffee together, those times of laughter, those times of weeping together, those times of just the quiet knowing we are loved that makes it all worthwhile. As I look once again at the picture of the small yellow peculator, it is not just the past memoires of my father drinking coffee in the early mornings, but living in the present and recognizing the love that my daughter-in-law and I have shared all these years.

Love is patient, love is kind. It does not envy, it does not boast,
it is not proud.
It does not dishonor others, it is not self-seeking,
it is not easily angered,
it keeps no record of wrongs.

I Corinthians 13:4-8 NIV

In the last chapter of this story on grief, "Potters Hand," I have captured the picture of my favorite moss covered clay flower pot. As I look back on the date of the story I believe this picture was taken in 2008, so many more layers of moss had been added, only giving it a beautiful description of the ancient. As the colors of life fuse together as a picture of life experiences the tool of thankfulness is a component of rare beauty and I would say the world is waiting for you to share your story of overcoming grief.

There are many scriptures in the Bible such as Psalm 30:5 that speak of sorrow and weeping. But the flip side of the weeping season is also so many passages that refer to joy and peace. That is my prayer for you dear reader, that you too will allow hope to arise. You will come to know this season of sorrow will pass and you also will look back and reflect how much richer life will be for you as you reach out to another in their journey in sorrow and bring a smile or kind and loving word.

Weeping may endure for a night,
But joy comes in the morning. Psalm 30:5 NKJV

CHAPTER 7

FORGIVENESS

In my own life, the hardest person I have ever had to forgive was myself. I don't think that is a good thing, but for me that seems to be the way it has been. All along my own journey I have had to rely heavily on this Shepherd of Heaven. When I find myself in this state of affairs, grief can come in degrees not very comfortable and at times it is as if my heart is just broken. So I have just learned to turn to Psalm 51 that always brings me hope. I will use just a few verses here.

Create in me a clean heart, O God,
And renew a steadfast spirit within me.
Do not cast me away from Your presence,
And do not take Your Holy Spirit from me.
Restore to me the joy of Your salvation,
And uphold me by Your generous Spirit.
The sacrifices of God are a broken spirit,
A broken and contrite heart-
These, O God, You will not despise.
Psalm 51: 10, 11, 12, & 17 NKJV

I have pondered over the scripture (love others like you love yourself). That can seem a bit boastful, but I have come to recognize that if we can't love ourselves, it will be a sure thing; it will be hard to love others with an open heart.

Jesus said to him, "You shall love the Lord your God with all your heart, with all your soul, and with all your mind. This is the first and great commandment. And the second is like it: "You shall love your neighbor as yourself.
Matthew 22:37-39 NKJV

For those of you who in childhood went to Sunday school and maybe even accepted Christ as your Savior but you have run far away, you might think there is no hope for me. I will come back and ask you a question? "Why are you reading this little book on grief? Down inside that broken heart of yours, there must be a glimmer of a candle that you are still loved.

As one walks though this journey called life there can be some situations that are so overwhelming in grief that the memory gets buried. Now trust me, it very likely will resurface later. It can be something others would consider insignificant, but for you the sorrow was deep. Life could seem to be on an even keel and all of a sudden the memory returns and with it the same grief and you are surprised at the depth of the sorrow. I will share with you one of my own stories of when a memory surfaced and I did walk through the grief and found there was freedom from the sorrow from the past.

THE BUTTERFLY BUSH

In the last planting season I came across a flowering bush in meanderings throughout my favorite garden nursery. It is called a butterfly bush, (Buddleia). I brought my new discovery home and planted it behind the multi-colored miniature mums next to the fence in the backyard.

In my daily evening practice of watering plants in my garden, I have taken great delight in watching the variety of butterflies floating above the long stems of puffy purple color stretching up and over the rest of the flowering plants. A few days ago when the late summer temperature was too hot to sit outdoors, I went out early in the morning.

I pulled a deck chair around behind the tall bush where I could be quiet and out of view. At first I did not pay attention to the butterfly bush, but then later I found myself gazing intently at it and found a solace, although there were no butterflies floating down from the sky on that morning with the heat already pressing down on me.

It had been a restless night with many bouts of crying as the dark hours of night slipped into morning. In times past this state I found myself was not unusual but my life has come into a place of balance so I have adapted tools of resiliency that can help me ward off the sadness. Last night the lid so tightly fastened to my jar of sorrows had been unexpectedly pulled off.

By now you the reader are wondering what is in this jar of sorrows? My answer to you is, "Don't we all have a story." Rather than draw you into my long and detailed book of woe, I turn and ask you, what is that sorrow you carry? Have you suffered a divorce, lost a child, been diagnosed with cancer? Has an injustice been done to you, shattering your sense of worth? Are you one of our faithful soldiers coming back from the war missing arms and legs wondering if you will be accepted? Or might you be that one setting in a prison cell with the memory of taking another life and you feel there is no way to overcome your own sorrow and with it the inability to ever come to a place you can forgive yourself.

It doesn't take much, does it, to bring us back to that place. The lid comes off, and with it, emotions we don't want to walk through one more time in life. It is often said that time is the great healer. I would come back with a response that time can only heal if we equip ourselves with tools to manage the sorrow and guilt. One more insight into my own journey, is I now recognize that for the rest of my life there will be times that a sadness will come to me, but for the most part it doesn't swamp me, but rather, I am challenged as I recognize how much quicker I come back into balance as time passes.

We tend to define life with those things relevant to ourselves, so because I am a seamstress I will use my personal example of elastic. In those early stages of grief we feel like that worn out elastic in an old pair of pants, all frayed with no stretch left to our spirit. But then as we gain strength the elastic becomes more usable, as if we replaced the old with new. I measure my wellness, not by emotions that can betray the strongest of us, but how quickly I can spring back when the elastic of my own life journey is stretched to its greatest endurance.

Each one of us has that part on the inside of us described as the soul, full of emotions and then there is the deepest place where our spirit dwells. That place the Shepherd of Heaven knows so well in each of us. But then he is the Son of God isn't he. I have known this Shepherd from the time I was a small child, and yet day by day I have to stand in awe at the compassion he is so willing to give, if only we take the time and realize how much he cares for the deepest sorrows that have come in life.

I think of the times when throngs of people swamped Christ as he walked along, yet he would see the beggar everyone else stepped over. The lepers who were left outside the city walls to die alone did not go unheeded by this Shepherd of Heaven.

The chorus from a song I sang as a young person comes to mind as I am penning words to the page this afternoon.

> "When Jesus comes the tempters power is broken.
> When Jesus comes the tears are washed away.
> He takes the gloom and fills the life with glory
> For all is changed when Jesus comes to stay."

If only we could count those things that are imparted to each of us freely from this Master of Heaven, but I do believe it would be impossible. I will speak of one gift I highly treasure and that is the ability to forgive. As we come with that burden too heavy to carry and lay it at the feet of Jesus, he not only gives us the ability to forgive others, but in turn he allows us the privilege to forgive ourselves. You might come back with, "But you don't know what this person has done to me, I can never forgive him/her." I would respond with as much compassion as is possible and tell you to not forgive will eat you alive.

I have often referred to the work of <u>Ruth Arent</u>, in working with hurting children. One of the very significant comparisons she tabulated through her years of research was "Hurt verses Hate." Unforgiveness is a hard task master that can bring the deepest of hurt and sorrow. Left unattended this hurt can spiral down into bitterness which in the end of the road can lead to hate which brings its own torment. *Ruth Arent, page 2

One of those components of learning to walk with God is the ability to have a conscience. As the seasons of my own life flow into the next horizon I have come to respect and honor the voice inside of me that is faithful to bring conviction when I mess up. The freedom and resiliency that comes from responding to that inner voice brings a peace in the greatest of storms.

Humanity is an interesting study, as some tend to swing from one pendulum to the other but most of us live somewhere in the middle. I'm speaking of the givers and the takers. Givers out of balance tend to not only forgive but take on the faults of another as their own. Thus we have the term all too familiar in our society as the co-dependent. Then there is the taker. The taker may be in the family or possibly in a very influential position. This person has very skillfully learned to place all responsibility on another. As time passes this person can become so toxic that they leave a wide path of destruction behind them wherever they go.

This is the person we find so hard to forgive as we feel we run right up and crash into a brick wall. But then what is the point of all this? When we come to the end of ourselves and ask the Spirit of God to come and gently give us a contrite heart, we are then blessed with this beautiful gift and it is the ability to forgive. And with this we also can begin to learn the important process of setting healthy boundaries. That is when true freedom comes, regardless what the other person does. With this comes a compassion for others in a state of flux hitting that brick wall.

Before our own experience of heartache it would be easy to pass by just like the throngs of people stepping over the beggar in the street.

At this point I refer back to the chorus I sang long ago, "Then Jesus Came." When Jesus touches a person's life in those areas so broken and brings peace that is when just a small glimpse of his glory shines down and brings hope.

Now let us go back to that butterfly bush I referred to previously. Sometimes when the great sadness returns we find ourselves alone trying to rise above the heaviness but then we are really never alone are we, as we know by scriptures that God is always there ready to come with his loving care. Hopefully, each of us in our own personal journey has those friends who just love us unconditionally. Usually compassionate people have had their own stuff they have had to work through, but they have learned through experience one of the greatest healing tools is to reach out to someone else and help them.

That hot summer morning gazing over at that butterfly bush was one of those times with me. As I sat there behind the side of the house, my heart felt so torn I found it hard to breath. I was surprised at how the sorrow had somehow hit me between the eyes with a deadly blow. I just humbled myself and called one of my faithful comrades, who understood, oh so well, what I was experiencing. She didn't feel sorry for me, the very last thing I needed at that point. "I know this hurts, you have a right to feel this sorrow, but you can face it. Now I know you can do it, just face the pain today. You can do!"
For the rest of day, sometimes even with tears running down my cheeks, "I would say, "I can do this."

When our conversation was over I wished that friend was present as I was so grateful to her, because I knew without a doubt that God had used her as his servant on that hot stifling morning.

When I put away my cell phone my gaze fell upon the butterfly bush nearby.

I saw the beautiful purple long stemmed flowers blowing gently overhead.

But then I looked behind the bush and saw the long stems heavy with flowers up next to the fence. I had walked by the bush everyday in my garden meanderings but had never taken the time to examine closely the large branch bent down to the ground.

I couldn't help but see the allegory between myself and the weighted down branch on the butterfly bush that day.

As we see in scripture, the Shepherd of Heaven never slumbers or sleeps. He is very cognizant of everything that touches our lives. I do not have answers for some things in life. I just know that He has always been faithful to come to me, sometimes in the worst of situations when I didn't know what to do.

Let me ask you again. "What is your story?" What is the situation in your life, you wish with everything in you, you could just wipe away like chalk on a blackboard? But it isn't chalk is it, it is real and it is your story, filled with sorrow and anger and everything else we each wish had never happened.

Time passes for each of us. Day by day and sometimes moment by moment if we can trust in faith to come to the cross and lay our sorrow at the feet of the Great Shepherd of Heaven he gives us tools we need to walk our own personal journey. And then one day the awareness comes that the very thing that brought so much heartache is the very thing that causes character to develop and we are given insight we would never have had before.

I have come to realize the flowers and fruit in my own life that have developed in those branches weighted so close to the ground have given me a keen sense of humanity and the ability to love the unlovely and for that I am most grateful.

Patricia Booher, November 16, 2010

NEAR THE CROSS
Jesus, keep me near the cross,
There a precious fountain-
Free to all, a healing stream-
Flows from Calvary's mountain.

In the cross, in the cross,
Be my glory ever;
Till my raptured soul shall find
Rest beyond the river.

Near the cross, a trembling soul,
Love and Mercy found me;
There the bright and morning star
Sheds its beams around me.

Francis Crosby, 1869

I have shared this story of childhood in the Shepherd book and Beloved Homeland, as it so portrays the love a father has for his child. I was thirteen when this happened and my goodness that is a long time ago. I will place it here as we speak of forgiveness and how important it is in walking through grief.

4-H Sheep Tragedy

The old lambing shed full of dust and shadow, would seem to give escape from the August blast of heat, but not on this late afternoon. The metal roof, turned to a burnt umber shade from years of Wyoming's brutal January cold and wind, was on this late afternoon, a sun baked oven for me as I worked steadily combing and carding the Colombia Ewe I would take to the county fair.

Summers on the McClaflin farm were filled with long hours of work and 4-H activities. My elder brother Mike, thirteen months older to be exact had a stack of purple ribbons on his bedroom wall from several years of having the great thrill of winning Grand Champion on his prize Hampshire pigs.

It wasn't my intent to compete with my brother but the lonely red ribbon from last year's Columbia ewe just didn't have the same place of prestige in my thirteen year old way of thinking.

The suffocating heat pressed down upon me on that afternoon but the words from my father kept me pressing on, steadily combing, carding, and combing again.

Several weeks prior, my father came in for dinner with that look on his face that clued me into to something exciting that was about to happen. "Well Pudden, I was out in the pasture and I saw your Colombia Ewe and checked her out. I think you have a Grand Champion there." That set the wheels rolling. This was my year. I had worked so hard on my 4-H sheep and now my time had come. There would be a purple ribbon on my bedroom wall, just on the east side where the afternoon's sun rays would show her off in all her splendor.

Living on a homestead near the east gate of Yellowstone Park was a draw for friends and relatives from afar. We were blessed with many guests in our home, probably because both Mom and Dad were such gracious hosts, in spite of the heavy work load they carried. Fair time was the busiest week of summer for our family, as we all participated in the 4-H judging activities. My father's Uncle Elmer and his wife, Aunt Lizzie had come the day before. I had spent some time with them last night after supper and then back out to the barn I went and worked late into the night. Mike would come out and check on me and help me some, but most of the time I quietly worked away on my Grand Champion, always with my Dad's words propelling me on.

My Columbia ewe patiently stood on the fitting stand, her head in a leather harness, as I worked with diligence hour after hour. The late afternoon sun was accompanied by 100 degree temperatures that left me dry and parched. The family was all in the house drinking iced tea and visiting with my elder relatives. I was tired. I was lonely and missing out on all the fun. My thirst reached an unbearable level of dustbowl proportion.

I quickly ran to the house, leaving my ewe harnessed to the stand. As I entered the kitchen, I could hear Uncle Elmer telling one of his many stories. I filled a large glass with ice cubes, let the cold water run to the top of the brim and then stood for a minute by the living room door. One minute turned into five, and then I knew I must run quickly back to my champion sheep.

It has been over sixty years since that late afternoon in August, but even now as I pen the words, I feel that same quickening of breath with what I found in the sheep shed that day.

The silence; where was that beautiful head of white wool? As I came into the wooden framed doorway, the first impact of tragedy was the harness pulled tight around her neck, taking the breath out of her body. She had fought against the tethered leather just enough to lose her footing and had fallen off the fitting stand.

I turned screaming with a cry of anguish. A cry from the very depths of me running as fast as my body could fly, "Daddy, Daddy!" The screen door flew open as my father ran through it, my brother close on his heels. Of course they both tried to resuscitate the beautiful prize winning sheep, but she was gone. There was no way to console that young girl with sun baked skin for many days to come.

The look on my father's face coming through the screen door has lived on with me and the recollection is burned upon my memory. The look of concern on his face has come to me at times when I have needed that same mercy and loving kindness from a Heavenly Father who is touched with compassion too for his people who cry out for a father when they least deserve it.

Patricia, January 2008

We are living in a time in which the family is going through great transitions and I dare say it is not for the better. Regardless of what society throws at us, the family from the very beginning of creation was God's plan. It is true that most of our greatest tragedies and triumphs are within the family.

For many years I taught a class on parenting, and why are you not surprised that the title of the class, regardless of the participants was always entitled, "Creative Parenting." The class was conducted with many groups and in a variety of settings. What is interesting to me, is after all these years and countless parents, I never had a parent come up after the class and say, "I am a good parent." It just doesn't happen. We as parents tend to remember those times we didn't do so good, forgetting the many times we probably did a good job of parenting and loved our children very well.

Now let me turn to you as you are about ready to put this little book down. You are feeling incredible grief right now because you cannot recall a father running through the screen door. Maybe you grew up without a father, or maybe he was cruel, broken and had addictions that caused him to turn on you many times.

Maybe you grew up without a loving mother. She had such brokenness herself she was not capable of nurturing and loving you. You have had to somehow keep going, but there will always be some portion of your heart that will ache, for we always want our parents to be there nurturing us throughout our life journey.

Then there is the child that had loving parents, but when you became a teenager, you went to the wild side. You have caused your parents so much grief, said things that should never be spoken, and there is no way you can ever take back those words. Maybe your parents have passed away and now there is just that deep hole in your heart.

Many times down through the years, I have found myself in the role of counselor. As I would listen to the stories of life from those young people with broken hearts, I would turn to this scripture;

When my father and my mother forsake me,
Then the Lord will take care of me.
Psalm 27:10 NKJV

If you have lived a life like the prodigal son, just go back home, hug your parents neck and humble yourself. Don't make excuses, just ask forgiveness. Remember the family was God's plan. We parents make our mistakes, but when it comes to our children, the river runs deep.

In just a few weeks we will be celebrating Easter. I can never thank God enough that he would send his son to us, knowing the cost of it all. I have pondered many times the night before Christ's crucifixion when he was in the Garden of Gethsemane all alone.

The disciples had all fallen asleep. It would be easy for the rest of us to condemn them. As I think about the tragedy of that night, I wonder if the foreboding of what was to come, not realizing the storm clouds of eternity were passing over, caused a heaviness to fall on the eleven. I am sure for the rest of their lives they wished many times, "Oh why didn't we stay awake with our Master in his darkest hours."

When Jesus spoke to the disciples, before the crucifixion of sending the Comforter, the Holy Spirit, they were not able to comprehend what he was saying to them; but then after he ascended into Heaven they would know this Comforter that always dwelt with them.

I have found the Comforter sent from Heaven is always present, and I do believe in those times of grief he seems to be even closer.

"Nevertheless I tell you the truth. It is to your advantage that I go away, for if I do not go away, the Helper will not come to you; but if I depart, I will send Him to You." John 16:7 NKJV

The year my sheep died passed into the next year. Another beautiful Columbia ewe was part of my flock and once again I found myself out in the sheep barn night after night never leaving the fitting stand for a moment.

It was sheep judging day at Park County Fair on that late August afternoon. There were a number of ewes lined up that day as I held onto the neck of my much loved Columbia sheep.

I just could not believe it! The judge was pointing to me to move my sheep to the front of the line. I was thrilled as I held for the first time a purple ribbon with the words falling down the side, "Grand Champion."

I took my sheep back into the dark shadowy sheep barn. The stall was almost to the end of the isle. I closed the gate tightly and turned around. "Where is my Dad?" I looked down to the wide barn door full of the late afternoon sun and saw a silhouette standing there. He strolled down the aisle and even in the dark shadows of the barn I saw tears in his eyes. I just ran to my Daddy and he swept me up and hugged me oh so tightly.

It has been sixty years now, since that day I held that purple ribbon in my hand. I keep it close to me in my little writing room over there on the shelves with my cherished books. I let the streamers hang down the side of the books, so I can always have it in view. It is wrinkled and faded, but I dare not iron it for fear it would just melt away. It is just an old faded ribbon from a county fair, but it is a treasure to me, as it holds the memories of an afternoon very long ago in a faraway place called Wyoming.

Well my dear reader, we have managed to get through this portion. I can tell you for sure, even after all these years, this chapter has not been written without some weeping, but I also feel joy that I do know this Comforter in such a tender way.

If you are in sorrow, let that father from Heaven who has been waiting oh so long for you to call out to him. Allow the Shepherd of Heaven to come quickly though screen door for you today.

Weeping may endure for a night, But joy comes in the morning.
Psalm 30:5 NKJV

Footnotes:

1. Hymn: "Then Jesus Came" Words by Oswald Smith, Music by Homer Rodeheaver, 1940.

2. Arent, Ruth, M.A., M.S.W., <u>Trust Building with Children Who Hurt</u>. The Center for Applied Research in Education, West Nyack, New York 10995, 1992.

    Hymn: "Near the Cross," Francis Crosby, 1869

CHAPTER 8

HUMOR, A RESILIENT TOOL

Those times of grief are not pleasant and in some circumstances the landscape of life will change forever. I think many times as parents we don't realize those attributes that are so important to our children. I grew up with a healthy sense of humor, not realizing my children loved to hear their mother's laughter. I used to laughingly say in most families parents entertain their children. In our family, I took such delight in my children that they would entertain me.

I went through a time of great sorrow some years back. My children and grandchildren lived in Michigan and I was in Wyoming. I made a point to be with them during the holidays. After one visit when I was able to just relax from the sadness, and found myself with that old laughter surfacing which the family had loved, my daughter-in-law, Sandy, told me what my son had said. "Now Sandy that is how I remember my Mom". That became one of those pivotal points in my own journey to have the determination to come out of grief and get on with life.

The death of my pet Timmy did take me onto another path in which I had not previously thought of. I have included this incident with the PJs as an example of humor in the midst of situations. I had just started the process of writing this manuscript, and my emotions were raw.

I found myself laughing so many times about those silly PJs; it would bring such a relief and new strength that would propel me on in writing.

HOW IS THE ELASTIC IN YOUR PJs

A few days ago I was having one of those delightful early morning breakfasts with my daughter before she was off to work. I was telling her how disappointed I was about the laundry room downstairs in my apartment complex. This incident was not as serious as I was making it out to be. I have felt so safe and at home in this apartment so I was having some of those thoughts of betrayal in my own corner of the world.

The day before, I had hurried through my list of chores in order to get in some writing. I took several loads of wash downstairs and didn't realize until I was folding the clothes later that evening that three pairs of PJs and my Eddie Bauer jeans were missing. I kept waking up in the night wondering what else I had washed in the afternoon that had been stolen. The next morning as I was drinking that first cup of coffee, I began to realize what a foolish thing to be so upset, although I did feel somewhat violated.

As far as the Eddie Bauer's, they had been saved from the times that we did have a waistline in pants. Now when I go try on jeans, somehow they seem to be designed for a thirteen year old bean pole, not a matronly grandmother such as myself, so that was a loss. But as for the PJs, I just had to break out in laughter. Who in the world would want three pairs of faded pajamas with elastic worn out that barely stayed on as I would climb into bed?

Later that morning as I went to pick up the white shirt to be ironed for work, I happened to notice at the bottom of the basket, another stash. Yes, all fretting and loss of sleep had been in vain, as there were all those items neatly folded from a few days earlier. I sheepishly thought I would need to call my daughter when she got home and apologize for worrying her.

By now you are asking yourself, what does this have to do with grief? Glad you asked. The sense of humor that has seen me through a lifetime of stuff was with me even as a young child. I have come to find out that a sense of humor can be a wonderful survival tool of resiliency or it can be a way of covering pain never dealt with.

Hopefully childhood is a time of happy memories for children. My brother Mike is just thirteen months older then myself. We were always the best of friends. Some of my happiest memories were the times we would create humor out of the basics of life. The homestead kids all knew how to work hard. There just was so much to be done and all the families lived frugal lives. I have observed that children can learn to create their own world of creativity and humor in this kind of environment. Those long days in the hot July sun we would be out in the bean field pulling weeds created a panorama of mischief, great weed fights and a great deal of laughter.

I am grateful to my Mom in that she taught me to laugh at myself. I was a sensitive child and have to admit I have not changed much, but I did take her advice and worked hard at being able to just see the humor in situations. This has worked out well for me with my grandchildren, as they take great delight in teasing their grandmother. It is never in a harsh manor, but they do get me laughing and that is a beautiful part of living and enjoying the children.

That isn't always the case, and sometimes it is later in life one walks through those heart aches long forgotten. If you grew up in a family void of humor, then you can be the one that creates that place in life where humor and just pure laughter of the enjoyment of life can be honored.

The negative side of humor is that it can be used in a sarcastic and cruel fashion to mask pain and verbally abuse others. Unfortunately this type of humor will not be a positive tool of bringing one out of the throes of grief and most likely will only increase the pain to one's self and to others.

I don't know if this is done any more, but years ago there would be TV programs in which some famous person would be roasted by friends. Needless to say I would always turn the channel to something else. I just could not see the humor in humiliating someone in front of the whole world. Of course the person being roasted had a smile on their face, but I pondered how they must have felt when the grueling night was over and everyone else went home.

"Humor is a universal language; everyone can relate to funny stories, pratfalls, and crazy antics. But humor can also be used as a serious technique to spur creativity and to solve problems. In addition, humor contributes to healing and good health." *Ayan, Page 136.

I have always believed that two of the best parts of life are children and our pets. All one has to do is look at the ratings on the Internet of funny antics of these two groups of creatures and the humor they can create can make one laugh on some of the worst days.

As so often happens as I am writing a memory of long ago surfaces. Such is the case with this snippet of life. My husband and I had flown from Manilla, Philippines south to Cebu City.

We stayed with a missionary couple, the Farrands, who were very special to us. We were conducting a family seminar for several days. I convinced them to let me bring my puppets along and lead the congregation in some scripture choruses. What was such a delight to me is that those families with their beautiful children would just erupt into joyous laughter. I have to say I fell in love with those families from the beginning. From that first morning service, when I would be out and about on the mission grounds, there would be small heads of children popping up from the dense tropical forest. After a time they would begin to follow me around wherever I went. So from that first encounter, if I would be out I would tuck one of the small hand puppets into my pocket and visit with children who took great delight in my antics.

You might be wondering why I would add this portion. I do believe it is very timely for our nation and all over the world, for that matter, as we have been through a difficult time in the last year with Covid. We have had masks on our faces, so communication and smiling at someone else has been impossible. Things are easing up now, but I am concerned as I am recognizing the fear that is still prevalent.

After so long, eye contact is not as it used to be. I am not going to give a political statement here, but I will ask the question, "What can I do to make a difference." Well, just as I have done in the past, I am going to put my cell phone away when I am out and about and just smile at others. The example of relating to those families so far away in the southern Philippians shows how quickly we can connect in a beautiful way to others, regardless of skin color or nationality.

Yes, the component of humor can truly be a tool to help each of us make a difference.

Jordan, Ayan, <u>AHA</u>! 10 Ways to Free your Creative Spirit and Find Your Great Ideas. Three Rivers Press, NY, NY, 1997.

CHAPTER 9

CREATIVITY

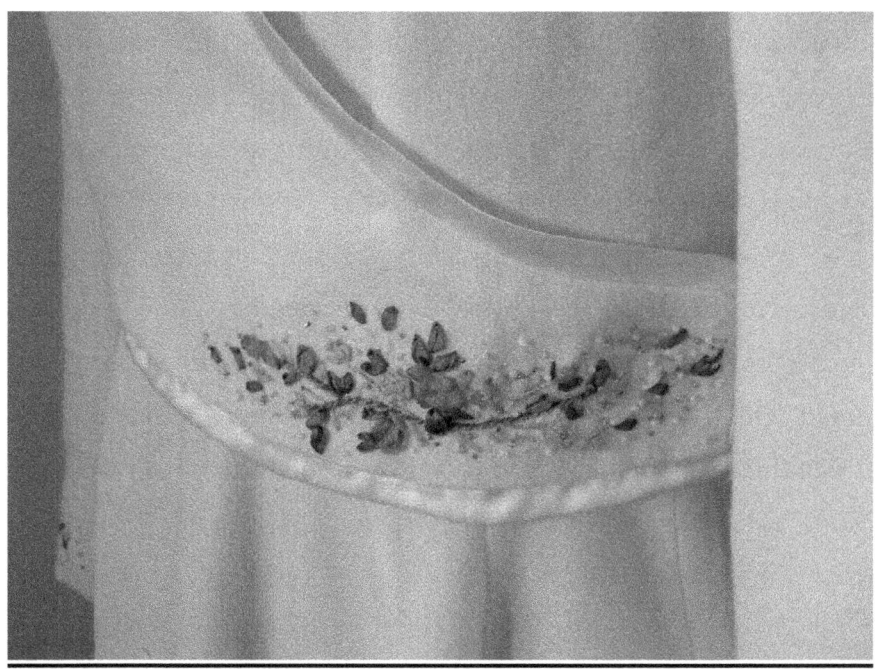

I have added the component of creativity in this story of grief as it has become a vital tool I have used most of my life. I am going to limit myself to just a few pages in this chapter, as my goal was to keep this book in small form and already the pages have moved beyond my original plan.

I have many wonderful stories on this topic of creativity and how important it can be in those times of grief. I will reserve most of those snippets for greater detail in the next book propelling me on to finish the last words of this narrative.

The non-fiction book will be entitled, "Creativity, Beauty Unfolding."

I have not made a list of acknowledgments in this narrative, but in this chapter on Creativity I am compeled to list three individuals who have opened doors of creativity within me that have added layers upon layers of resilient tools that have enriched my life. Edna McBreen, State Director of Wyoming Cooperative Extension allowed me to attend the Creative Problem Solving Institute in Buffalo, New York. This opened up a whole new world of Creativity that I formally was not aware of. Mary Martin was my colleague in Wyoming Cooperative Extension Service when I first came back to Wyoming. She introduced me to many forms of embellishment and quilting through "Quilting in the Tetons" she conducted for a number of years. Dr. Ben Silliman, Family Life Specialist, introduced me to many facets of Family Resiliency. Many of the research books in my stash I cherish were introduced to me by Ben.

Those years while on staff with the University of Wyoming the skills I was able to enhance evolved into giving classes and workshops on this topic of Creativity. I would have to say the highlight of it all was when I taught for a time in Saratov, Russia. The topics I taught were on Creativity and Leadership. There are countless forms of creativity that enrich our lives. If you are one of those who says you have no creative ability, then you need to hang around someone like me. Creativity can be a valuable asset as we walk through those times of grief. Writing, designing and gardening have been three of those outlets of creativity for me forever so long now. There is so much I could add to this chapter on creativity, but I just wanted to encourage you the reader, in whatever aspect of creativity you enjoy to put it to good use as you walk through your own times of sorrow and grief.

One of my greatest pleasures is to be with a group of small children and have a stash of paints and all kinds of textures. I give just a few simple guidelines, and then watch them from day to day begin to grow with confidence in what they create.

I will briefly mention one example of applying creativity with wounded children. My Colleague, Teddy Jones and I were conducting an "Anger Management" workshop with some troubled youth. Before we began each session we placed in front of them blank poster board with multi-colors of markers. I explained the technique of "Moodgee Drawing." I was introduced to this valuable creative tool from <u>Jon Pearson's</u> book. There were three sessions and by the last day, it was rewarding to see how the young people were able to relax and some of art work was amazing.

I want to point out that this is not a crutch. In fact, if this tool is used to mask the pain, the spiral only goes downward and can become destructive even addictive. I have said this line repeatedly throughout the chapters, but will say it again. I found in my own situations and grief, I just had to "head into the wind." I had to face the pain of it all and be honest with myself and see where I needed to grow and let God give me courage and faith that somehow I would make it through the storm.

There are many tools of coping with grief. I have chosen to list the combination of Forgiveness, Thankfulness, Humor and Creativity as healing tools that can bring into balance one's emotions and clarity in dealing with grief.

Yesterday, I took a reprieve from the daily writing and spent the day organizing and planting the flowers, herbs and vegetables in the flower pots on my beautiful deck. By last evening, I knew I had probably worked too many hours. But I have come to know that in the summer and fall seasons the garden patch whether in the backyard, apartment deck or now by the lake side is like a balm of peace and joy to my heart and soul.

I will forever be thankful for my friend Mary Martin, who just would not give up on me. I finally just gave into her and attended that first "Quilting in the Tetons." I will save that experience for the book on Creativity. Needless to say, how could I have ever dreamed how it has changed my life? The countless quilts I have made are really a work of creative art. Mary was one of those many friends and family members who were in the wings cheering me on when the writing of poems began and then came the stories that turned into books. On and on the story can go.

I have inserted the waistline of the wool dress I made for my mother before she passed away. The details of beads, intricate stitching and silk ribbon flowers were all techniques I learned through the years attending the conference in Jackson Hole Wyoming.

We know one day we will say good-by for the last time to our parents, but that does not stop the deep sorrow that goes with it. In those days as I would design, sew and think of my Mom's face when she saw the dress I grieved at losing her. The beauty in all of it is I was able to process the steps of grief in those months of sewing and so I say it was a blessing.

This morning as I was bringing this chapter to a close, I thought about that first writing journal now yellow with age. I went to the shelf and saw that I have put colored tape on the binding as there are many journals I have saved through all these years. As I opened to the first page that is tattered and torn I first noted the date. This was just a few weeks after that life changing time for me, recovering from the car wreck. As you read the lines of this simple but profound poem you might be saying, "I could not write this poem as right now my heart is raging with grief." I just want to encourage you now that you might be way up in years and have never let the Shepherd of Heaven come along side, but dear one he has waited so long to tell you he loves you and his heart is touched with your grief.

As you have read through these snippets of my journey, it is evident that there have been many mountain tops and deep valleys I have crossed. Oh truly there were times of grief, I did not know if I would make it, but I just kept running to the Shepherd of Heaven. I describe in the "Forgiveness" chapter as the Daddy running through the screen door.

QUIETNESS

Be still quiet heart and listen.

Listen to the gentle, peaceful stillness;

The gentle stillness where Christ can be found.

His presence is a balm to the hurting.

His kindness is the light at the end of the tunnel.

His joy is the courage that keeps me ever pushing forward.

His friendship is the kernel of hope that gives me value.

His character is what I want my life to dissolve into.

March 3, 1994

It seems time has a way of repeating itself; but with the added component of creativity it has the capacity to bring a rich tapestry of beauty even in the deepest sorrow. If I were to describe creativity in a person's life, it would be as a circle that is never ending. And then I would see a circle within a circle stretching out into the beyond of this present time.

Pearson, Jon, <u>Drawing on the Inventive Mind</u>. P.O. Box 25367, Los Angeles, California, 90025, 1995.Page 35.

SECTION III

EVERYONE HAS A STORY

CHAPTER 10

CUP HALF FULL/CUP HALF EMPTY/YOUR CHOICE

I remember a family reunion many years ago that was going to be up in the mountains near Collbran, Colorado with Dave and Barbra Booher. When I look at the map this morning, I realize this little town was way off the beaten path. There was an old log cabin with a small creek running nearby. The old barn had some horses which was my great delight. Our three children were very young at the time, so although I loved being in the mountains, I was very busy watching over them.

This morning as I am writing, I reminisce as I think of that trip. This happens often when I am writing. A little snippet of a story of life just seems to emerge out of long ago memories.

When we were growing up on the McClaflin homestead, my brother Mike milked the cow every morning. My job was to pasteurize the milk. I would bring the large glass jug into the kitchen and put it in the refrigerator. It would not take long for the cream to begin to rise to the top.

My mom was one of those homestead wives that could whip up the most amazing meals. In those days we made everything from scratch. There were three big meals a day. Many times hired men would be sitting at our kitchen table with the family. At a very early age I was cooking right along with my Mom.
I began baking very early in my life and it seems to be the station I still find myself in.

When I got married I had to make a big adjustment, as all the recipes for cakes, biscuits and whatever usually were made with the cream that rose to the top.

As we drove to the reunion that summer we stopped at my husband's parents' home out in eastern Colorado. Dad had just gotten a beautiful Jersey milk cow. As I got into the car to leave he handed me a quart jar of cream. I had not been able to bake with cream for several years. This was a gift I took great delight in and immediately began to make plans.

Every morning I would get up and bake a big batch of biscuits using the cream. One relative said he didn't like biscuits. I said, "Well why don't you just try one of these made with cream from off the farm" Needless to say, he was the first in line for the biscuits for the rest of the reunion.

CREAM OF THE CROP

I often jokingly use the comment when conversing with another person or in teaching, "I am going to be happy if it kills me." Except I am not joking, I am completely serious in this attitude of looking at life with my cup half full. It hasn't always been this way. There have been times I have worked really hard on this attitude. As I have referred to earlier; one component that is necessary is just the simple attitude of being thankful. I haven't always been thankful in the past for circumstances that have brought incredible grief to my life, but in looking back and seeing the kindness that has been shown to me and the faith and trust in God that grew out of that period of my life; I would have to say, I have had a life blessed in so many ways.

In my small library room where I am writing today, I look over and smile as I recognize my many research type books I have gathered through the years. Some are worn with use. They are my own stash, so many of them have pages folded down, sticky notes that can be easily seen for reference, highlights and more highlights on top of the old. I have gained many tools of coping with grief and just understanding life from the research found in those books. Of course, the book that is always on top of the pile as I write is the Bible in many different translations.

Looking back on my own childhood, I recognize that the 4-H Youth Program had a significant impact on every aspect of my life. In our homestead community many of the parents were very involved as leaders and 4-H was a part of everyday life. Even after we were grown our parents' continued on investing in young people.

When I grew up I didn't get to go back home to Wyoming very often. I had bouts of homesickness, missed my parents and friends and the mountains that I had loved as a child.

It is interesting to me, those conversations when spoken don't seem to impact one, but we find later that we remember them as if yesterday. One of those times as a young mother while sitting with my dad, I remember his comment in passing. "Pat you always want to invest in young people." Hopefully I have taken his words to heart in my own life.

Growing up in a homestead community we were surrounded in an agriculture atmosphere.

I soon came to realize in a large city like Detroit, I was far removed from the common place every day descriptions I had grown up with.

The 4-H Youth Program challenged young people in so many ways. We were often referred to as the "Cream of the Crop." Now for a city dweller, that has no significance, but for those of us who drank coffee and made early morning biscuits with cream that rose to the top of the jar, we knew exactly what it meant.

In those teaching years in the Detroit area, I came to realize there were students sitting in my classroom, that were not given the privileges of childhood I had taken for granted. There was just some kind of radar inside of me that wanted to see all my students as "Cream of the Crop."

STAGES OF LIFE

Many years ago I came across research conducted by Erik Erikson which relates to the eight developmental stages of life. I have his book, "<u>Childhood and Society</u>," sitting among my many books I refer to often.

ERIK ERIKSON'S STAGES OF LIFE DEVELOPMENT

Basic Trust vs. Basic Mistrust   Infancy (birth to 18 months)
Autonomy vs. Shame and Doubt   Early childhood (2 to 3 years)
Initiative vs. Guilt   Preschool (3 to 5 years)
Industry vs. Inferiority   School age (6 to 11 years)
Identity vs. Role Confusion   Adolescence (12 to 18)
Intimacy vs. Isolation Young Adulthood (19 to40)
Generativity vs. Stagnation   Middle Adulthood (40 to 65)
Integrity vs. Despair Maturity (65 to death)

In my own stash of research and significant works done down through the generations on the human frame, I would not infer that it is written in stone that each person will go through <u>Kubler-Ross</u>'s five steps of grief. Every person is unique and every life circumstance makes its own impact on the individual. In many ways we humans have more similarities than differences. I have found Erikson's research helpful in understanding myself, but more importantly as I relate to others, putting into perspective why and how they react to life.

Today as I am writing, a former high school student comes to mind. I will not divulge his name, honoring his privacy I just trust that someday he might pick up this book and remember the day I am bringing back into my own remembrance.

I had come back to school that September after the death of my father, going through the motions, but not with the same zest I had previously had, as teaching was one of the joys of my life.

There was a young man, who was acting out and if he couldn't pull himself together, he was going to be expelled. I had sketches of his story. When he was a young boy his father had been killed. I hoped he was not with his father when this happened. I cherished all my students, but I found in this young man, something special and unique. As I observed him from day to day, it would seem as if I looked down into his heart.

One day there was a cancellation of one of my classes just after lunch. That gave me almost two hours and I thought of this young man. There was a nice restaurant just a few blocks away. I asked him if he would like to go have lunch with me. I was amused as he ordered and I took great delight as I watched him enjoy his food.

If I can recollect correctly, I think he ordered a big hamburger, French fries, Pepsi, and cherry pie. I sat there praying under my breath for wisdom. I began to tell him how sad I was at the death of my father, and felt I somehow understood him. Even as he ate his lunch tears began to run down the sides of his face. He just began to pour out his heart telling about his dad and how much he missed him.

To console those who mourn in Zion,
To give them beauty for ashes, The oil of joy for mourning,
The garment of praise for the spirit of heaviness;
That they may be called trees of righteousness,
The planting of the Lord, that He may be glorified.
Isaiah 61:3 NKJV

I didn't go through the five steps of grief with him. I didn't counsel him. I just listened to him and then we both cried together. It wasn't a quick fix for that young man. I just have to believe that just knowing there was someone else walking through their own process of grief and was willing to take the time to look beyond the behavior and see his heart that day. Hopefully in time, as he remembered that lunch conversation, it would give him the courage and hope that he would get through that stage and go on and have hope for his future.

When it comes down to it, life is a choice. Each person walks through those stages of life, and depending on how they are willing to grow and sometimes through great obstacles, their life can be fruitful. I am surprised at how quickly the years have moved through those seasons for me.

I have always had the practice of placing my name and date of purchase on that first page of books I purchase.

I do believe that for most of my life, I have questioned and observed not only in myself, but others what makes one person give up while another seems to rise above the circumstance, no matter how great the challenge.

One of those books I have poured over and it is evident, is "Adversity Quotient, Turning Obstacles into Opportunities." As I reflect, I had this book as one of my favorites for several years before I faced some challenges in sickness and also grief. As my fingers are walking through the pages, I am reading so many highlighted passages and research. This brings a foundation to this aspect of facing grief with courage; I will focus in on just a few portions. The author speaks of three categories of persons facing obstacles: Quitters, Campers, and Climbers.

The author states, "Of these three types of people, only Climbers live life fully. They feel a deep sense of purpose and passion for what they do. It is the climbers faith that somehow things can and will be done despite the negativism of others who have determined that a certain route is impossible." They have the capacity to see life with a cup half full. *Stoltz, Page 18.

Campers have started up that mountain of courage, but about halfway up they decide to stay in camp. Depending on the degree of grief one is walking through it can appear at some point to just stay put in camp, as facing into winds of adversity can become brutal, but just to keep going and reach the top is where we can look back on our journey and have a grateful heart, knowing the courage it took.

Quitters allow those challenges faced in life to become the central focus.

They give into whatever hardship seems insurmountable and unfortunately this can cause them to become stuck right there which will affect the rest of their journey in this life. They approach life with an attitude of their cup being half empty.

From the time I was a young child, I seemed to have a sense of God as a loving father. There were many times I felt his presence to such a depth it was hard to contain the magnitude of it all. In turn I grew to have a deep devotion that has been with me throughout my own journey. I also recognize that many, even in this season of life have not had this privilege, and so for me to give up has never been an option. If I can come along side of another and give them courage to keep climbing their mountains then my life has been of worth.

Just like that young man I sat across from that day as he told of his father and how he had loved him, I have prayed many times that he would make good choices in his own journey in life and that he would be one of those young people just like the "Cream of the Crop."

I have come to realize that we can be an encourager. We can reach out, such as I trust these stories of my own journey will give courage to face hardship. But the final choice is up to each of us to decide if we will live life with the attitude of a cup half full or a cup half empty.

I will close this portion with these words, as I seem to express myself more easily through writing poems.

CHOICES

The longer I walk through this journey of life,

I realize the power I possess within to make choices:

Choices daily, sometime minute by minute,

Great personal courage and faith at times are necessary.

When I make choices where there are sacrifices,

When I choose love over hate,

When I choose forgiveness over holding on to Unforgiveness,

When I choose to look beyond myself to see that one who needs my caring,

Yes, life is a choice. So soon my days will pass.

What will I leave behind?

Dear God. Give me the courage to choose goodness

Patricia Booher, October 22, 1996

Erikson, Erik H. Childhood and Society. W.W. Norton and Company, New York, 1963. Pages 247 – 269.

Stoltz, Paul G. Adversity Quotient Turning Obstacles into Opportunities. John Wiley and Sons, Inc. New York, 1997. Pages 18-20.

CHAPTER 11

GRIEF AND TRAUMA

At this point in my own journey on this earth, I can't say I am really surprised at the memories that seem to surface as I write. This morning I woke very early to pray and then fell back to sleep for a period of time. When I awoke it seems I was back in the homestead home I grew up in as a child. This morning, it seemed so real as I look over at a picture of my father just a month before he died. It is so faded now; I have to look carefully to see that smile on his face as we looked at each other.

He left our family too quickly, but the Lord did bless him in the short time he had left as he wanted to speak to each of his children. That last night in June when we had gone to visit, he called me back into his bedroom. By then the cancer had filled his body, but the words he spoke that night come to me this morning. How appropriate, as in just a few years I would be heading into some storms of life that could have easily destroyed me.

My daughters had followed me back into his bedroom. He got into bed and we all laid down there beside him. "Pat you never give yourself credit. You reward everyone else for your accomplishments, but it always was your courage. I know it was hard for you to go back to college, but now here you are with a master's degree."

Yes, I think my dad did have some semblance of how very difficult it was. Just a few months earlier he and Mom had come back to Michigan for my graduation.

I am sure as I walked across that stage to get my diploma he was crying. My dad was a very quiet but insightful man. I do think he had a sense that I was heading into a storm of life. I think there were many midnight times of study when I was so sad and weary the only thing that kept me going was my faith in God and the look on my dad's face when I walked across the stage.

So now this morning, I am coming along side of you and I have a sense that you have something in your life that has kept you stuck. You dread the next time you have one of those nightmares when you relive whatever has happened to you. You feel isolated in your circumstances. You feel you are holding up the ship, so you dare not tell anyone what is going on in your life. But dear one, at this point I believe you would not be reading this book, if you didn't really want to walk out of this torment that saps your strength. There is a point one needs to ask for help. At times in my own journey, I would come across a book that would give me some courage to just keep pressing on. Of course, the main stay in my life was scripture that at times seemed to just clear the path in front of me.

In my stash of books I have many self-help books. Those books have given me tools in coping strategies for life. But at the end of it all no tool can heal a broken heart. So many times I have prayed Psalm 51. "Lord create within me a new heart." And yes, that is what my faith has done for me. God in his tender mercy has come to me so many times. As I have climbed my own mountains of adversity, I can look back and see I am not a quitter. No, I am not a camper. I am a climber!

This morning I am saying to you, "Yes give yourself credit, you are doing this, you are reading this little book; you want to be able to cope with your grief. You want to move through those stages of life, not beaten down, but like the eagle that sours high above the clouds. If you will whisper a prayer to this God of the universe, he will come to you. He has waited ever so long for you to call to him."

The grief and fear that come out of those times of trauma, or other circumstance that bring such incredible sorrow are hard to bring into balance. If one thinks they can just stuff the trauma down and forget it, well it does seem to resurface at a later time and sometimes the pattern becomes like a worn out record with the groove so deep one can feel helpless and in time this pattern turns into hopelessness. Maybe a more appropriate example would be a video played over and over with no turn off button.

When my friend Teddy and I conducted Anger Management workshops during our careers with the University of Wyoming Cooperative Extension, I have mentioned previously, after a time, we came up with the title, "Tiger in Your Tank." Now this was not our creation as I see many advertisements with similar titles. As we introduced this workshop to a variety of groups, we were careful to stress, this was not a class to be taken to deal with violent anger. Rather, it was information dealing with positive ways to recognize and handle anger in a non-destructive and even positive manner.

"One of the main indicators of trauma may be part of a person's life in experiencing the trauma. Thoughts and pictures of what occurred in the form of dreams, nightmares, or even flashbacks may take up residence in your life.

Sometimes they slip into your mind like a video stuck on continuous replay. This sensitivity can become so extreme that it even can trigger a flashback and make you feel and act as if you were experiencing the original trauma all over again. Again and again trauma interrupts life. It stops the normal process of life by its constant intrusion." *Wright, page 84.

Depending on the particular circumstance in your personal life, trauma can interrupt healthy advancement of growing through those stages of life I refer to in Erikson's research. At this point, if you are feeling that dread of how you have been impacted, I just want to encourage you. Ask yourself, "Why did I pick up this little book?" Take heart dear one, even by the second portion of the title, even though you might feel helpless to your past, there must be buried down inside of you that portion of faith that has been given to every human God placed on this earth. You might be someone who says, "I don't believe there is a God." Well we just won't worry about that right now.

In fact there is a God and he had you in mind before you were in your mother's womb. He has walked along side of you all of your life, loving you, feeling your pain, and recognizing that fear and foreboding that has gripped you forever so long now. I cannot give a rational explanation of the Bible. I just know through countless testimonies and my own life experience, that every verse has been inspired by the Holy Spirit. There is a power and healing balm for every fear and tragedy known to mankind.

I often listen to old hymns I have loved from childhood, as I am doing today writing this portion.

For you see, dear reader, writing the words in this chapter requires a whole lot of faith on my part that I won't slip down into that fear and sadness that can come on me as well. Throughout my own life, through every storm, I was gaining faith and a resiliency, so that at this point, I know what to do when a nightmare awakens me and that melancholy seems to just seep into my spirit.

If you are like me, you have had to be independent. You didn't have the privilege of leaning on someone else. I put it this way. "No matter what just get up and put on your marching boots and get going with the day." I have done that countless times, but then one day, I could no longer get up. I have written about the car wreck in the Shepherd book so I won't go into the details of it now.

The blessing that came out of that night is I know it was only a miracle I lived through the experience. Another side of the picture is that those things that once were an everyday luxury changed, so now as I write, I pray for strength and the Lord always comes to give me what I need for each day.

If you are at a place where the trauma is taking over your everyday life, you will need to reach out to someone to walk along with you. I have found that most of us want that one to be a family member. Sometimes that happens, but depending how severe the damage done to you, your family might not be equipped to handle the trauma or maybe you don't have family. This little book is not going to be a counseling session for you. Rather I have just come along side, knowing how far I have come and I want to encourage another.

 I have shared snippets of my own journey. I have been surprised at some portions I have been willing to share.

Well maybe not. You the reader have probably already understood there are volumes of life between the lines, but then we don't have to tell every little detail of heartache and trauma. That can be a trap for as we rehearse each and every detail, and those around us have it memorized as well, we find that we are not climbers, but have stopped on the mountain of endurance and maybe you just quit long ago.

Once again, before you put this little book down, the very point that you have gotten this far in the reading should give you courage. There must be a spark of hope down deep inside that you want to get over your sorrow. I came to a point in my own journey I knew I only had two choices. I could live out the rest of my life as a victim or get well.

For I know the thoughts that I think toward you, says the Lord,
thoughts of peace and not of evil,
to give you a future and a hope.
Jeremiah 29:11, NKJV

I have many portions of scripture that have become a part of the fiber of my life, but three chapters that I still read on a consistent basis are Psalm 51, Psalm 91 and Psalm 37. David the psalmist was a shepherd boy. He was a worshipper sitting out there on the hill side watching over those lambs, so maybe that is one reason I so relate to him.

He who dwells in the secret place of the Most High
Shall abide under the shadow of the Almighty. I will say of the Lord,
"He is my refuge and my fortress; My God, in Him I will trust."
Psalm 91:1-2. NKJV

I could continue on in this vain, but feel I must bring this portion to a close. And yet, in life there really never is a close, even after we have taken our last breath. As I look down through the ages of time we have records of those who have made an imprint on mankind for evil. This morning as I am sitting with you, and maybe you are in a lonely place, take on hope. I do believe those in humanity and even in the animal kingdom like my precious little pet, Timmy, who make the greatest impact are those who have brought courage to another. They have taken time to believe in the worth and value God has placed on each of us.

In closing this portion I want to encourage you to look over the books I have listed here. I chose not to weigh heavily on each topic they have so well researched, but to be a resource to merely bring to your attention their work. Alan Wolfelt has made great strides in furnishing support for those who desire healing and hope. This might just be a starting point for you, but then each of us have a beginning line written into the sands of time for our own race and maybe this is the first day of the rest of your life.

Peck, Scott. People of the Lie. Simon and Schuster, 1983.

Peck, Scott. The Road Less Traveled. Simon and Schuster, New York, 1978.

Seamands, David A. Healing for Damaged Emotions. Chariot Victor Publishing, Colorado Springs, Colorado, 1991.

Wolfelt, Alan D. Ph.D. Understanding Your Grief. Companion Press, Fort Collins, Colorado, 2003.

Wright, H. Norman, Experiencing Grief. Broadman and Hollman Publishers, Nashville, Tennessee, 2004, Page 84.

CHAPTER 12

DEEP CALLS TO DEEP

It had been hot and humid for days. Sleep did not come easily in the upstairs bedroom. The rain came in the night and with it the cool breeze that brought rest and the ability to wake early to the predawn stillness.

Those first moments of uncluttered thoughts were sharpened with an awareness of God's spirit hovering near my bedside. Although the room was gray with the overcast mist pressing down in its stillness. Night was over for me.

I went to my special sunroom where I pray. This morning the

golden rays were not flooding in the east window, but the cool breeze was a welcome to me.

I opened my Bible to Isaiah and began to soak in those words filled with faith and power of God's greatness. As I read down through the verses of Isaiah 61, I could feel the pull of the Holy Spirit in that deep place in my soul.

I paused to look up and saw a robin red breast looking down into my room from a pinnacle at the very top of the garage roof. Not wanting to sound mystical, but there have been many times throughout my life at pivotal points there has been a robin red breast that comes and places himself right in front of my path. I wouldn't say I can describe any spiritual application, but it has happened so many times down through the years, that I pay attention.

As I concentrated on the bird perched up at the highest point of the garage roof, a squirrel digging under the flowers next to the west window drew my attention away for a moment. When I glanced back at the garage the robin was gone. I knew God was speaking to that deep part of me, and for a moment I was frustrated at my lack of concentration. All of a sudden, there was a robin once again flying down and taking his position at the pinnacle point at the top of the garage. This is one of those points in my own life where I will need more faith then I have ever needed before to overcome those obstacles in my path. If I allowed myself to sink down into despair, tears of frustration and fear could rob this quiet moment of misty cool morning rain.

As the quiet voice of God came to me, I remembered that I had strength last evening to clean and wash down my upstairs deck.

I took my Bible and went up and pulled out the deck chair and sat up above the business of life looking down over roofs and gardens. No one was about, so the silent cool breeze was rejuvenating. As I was looking out over the garden and flowers in my neighbor's yard I saw another robin perched on the very top point of the house in the next yard.

This early morning experience with the robins makes me think of Samuel as a young child. I turned to I Samuel 3 and read the account of the small child who had been placed in the care of Eli the Priest.

What precedes this for me is Samuel's mother Hannah. As I read the prayer she prayed in gratitude to God for blessing her with this son, I was struck with her insight into the knowledge of the greatness of God. She had grieved so long for a child. The heart of Eli the priest was touched as he heard the desperate weeping of this woman he did not know. He prayed a blessing over her and her heart's desire was fulfilled when Samuel was born. One would think that after waiting so long for this child she adored with all of her heart, she would want to experience every stage of his growth; those first words, the young personality unfolding, looking at all of his homework, watching him play in little league. Actually this is one of those Bible stories that has always hit that soft spot in me as a mother.

One will have to read between the lines about this woman. I think if one pauses and carefully examines the prayer of gratitude she prays, we can assume she was a woman of faith and courage. These attributes were obviously passed on to Samuel as he became a prophet of God in the most difficult of times as a spiritual darkness had settled over the Lord's people.

Now the boy Samuel ministered to the Lord before Eli. And the word of the Lord was rare in those days; there was no widespread revelation. And it came to pass at that time, while Eli was lying down in his place, and when his eyes had begun to grow so dim that he could not see, and before the lamp of God went out in the tabernacle of the Lord where the ark of God was, and while Samuel was lying down, that the Lord called Samuel, And he answered, "Here I am!"
I Samuel 3:1- 4 NKJV

In the midnight hours when the voice of God was calling this young boy Samuel, he thought it was Eli the priest. Three times the voice called to Samuel. By that time Eli recognized it was God's voice calling this young boy. The message given to Samuel would be a heavy weight on this young lad, yet he was faithful in what he was called to do in relaying to Eli the message from the Lord.

The life of Samuel is an example of what can be possible to accomplish in the Kingdom of God, if one is willing to just listen to that voice from God and then have the courage to walk out his instructions.

This morning was one of those times for me. That silent voice I know so well, was speaking before I was even awake. I have often pondered the words

"Deep calls unto deep at the noise of Your waterfalls;
All Your waves and billows have gone over me.
Psalm 42:7 NKJV

This morning as the thoughts came so rapidly to me, I went to the old writing journal, yellow with age at this point, and looked up the words penned so long ago. I remember well that time in my life when all I knew to do every morning was just get up, put on my marching boots, so to speak, and just keep walking. From the very beginning of writing, if I had not placed a date at the end of the poem or story I would not be able to remember later when it was written. This was one of the first poems that came from that deep place in my soul

It was at such a time when the winter had almost passed I made my trek up to the Shell Falls in the Big Horn Mountain range in Wyoming, just a few minutes from my home. The rocks were heavy laden with huge blocks of ice and the clear dark water in the deep canyon was a beautiful sight. It was one of those grieving times for me that was a pivotal point in my own walk with God. A time that required more faith then former seasons of walking this life journey. This simple poem which I found in that first yellow journal of writings, written so long ago, came to me in that early morning just a few days before I would undergo surgery, not knowing if it would be cancer.

DEEP CALLS TO DEEP

The winter time of the soul, brings a heaviness of Spirit.
It brings loneliness and despair. like heavy snow on a waterfall,
Is the weight of this season.
But out of the deep dark and cold pools of winter,
Comes new life and joy.
And after a season of discipline comes spring.
May 26, 1994

Today I face new challenges that will require greater faith, coupled with humility of soul more than I have ever relied on before. But this is not a winter time season of the soul for me, but rather a time, I know I must stretch and listen keenly to that voice of God going before me to clear a wide path. Actually I find myself rejoicing, knowing how the Lord loves his children in such a way he would even send little robin red breasts three times in the early morning mist just as a reminder he is the Shepherd of Heaven.

As I sat there on my upstairs deck high above view in the quiet of this morning, I read once again one of my most favorite passages of scripture in Isaiah 61. Oh how I have cherished those times in my life when God's Spirit rested on me. What a privilege it has been walking this life journey out hearing this silent voice from Heaven guiding me through every valley and mountain trail

I think about those dear ones, who do not even know that God speaks to them as well. Others have begun their own journey in this walk with God, but circumstances have left them with a broken heart. They cannot face today, tomorrow seems as if it will never come, as the past has brought them to that deep place of the soul.

It is at a time like this, when the hard times come, yet there is peace and calm, that we are reminded to come along side that other passerby. As we fall into the tender arms of our Heavenly Shepherd, he can give us the grace to allow the Holy Spirit to shine like a light in darkness, bring beauty out of ashes, and remind that other hurting soul you are walking along side by side with them.

July 15, 2011

CHAPTER 13

CAR WRECK IN SHIRLEY BASIN

I drove away from home that morning with relief, as I saw the sun filtering down through the clouds. I was hoping the rays of amber, layered with a soft mist of pink cotton candy softness, were a promise of a warmer day then it had been in this northern Wyoming country in early February. I was in for a brutal surprise that would forever change my destiny and with this, a passion for life that would ever drive me on.

I was an Extension Educator with the University of Wyoming. My office was housed in the county courthouse in Big Horn County, in the town of Basin, right at the base of the massive and rugged Rocky Mountains. I lived in the small hamlet of Shell, and from the picture windows in my living room I could see right into the canyon, a wonderful place to live for someone like me who loved the beauty of nature.

The university was in Laramie, which was approximately a seven-hour drive from my home. Traveling was an ongoing part of my job, as I found myself many times all over the state doing programs. Because I was so used to long trips, I had pondered for days why I had such an unsettled feeling. I had called my mother several days before, asking her to pray for me, as I couldn't shake this uneasiness. I had a habit of rising early to watch the sunrise coming up over the mountains, as I didn't want to miss the splendor of such beauty.

The Sunday morning I was to leave, I was up at five, long before I would see the first gray glimpse of dawn. As I sat in my chair, with my gaze fixed on the eastern skies, sadness came over me. Although it wasn't an option, I just wished that I could stay home. Finally around seven, I finished loading my bags in the car and returned to lock the front door. This wasn't a usual custom, but on that morning, I opened the door, looked around to my familiar things, and said, "Good-by, little home." I started my Toyota Camry and headed down the hill and began my long trek to Laramie. On my many journeys, there was a familiar awareness that angels would accompany me. I would pray that the Lord would send angels to travel along with me, and this morning was no different.

As I drove through the town of Basin, I realized I had to get hold of this melancholy mood, or it was going to be a very long day. I reached into my stash of recordings and pulled out a tape of sermons from my daughter Shana, who lived in Seattle. On a regular basis, she would send me tapes of her pastor, Reverend Steve Schell of Northwest Foursquare Church. The topic was on praying many kinds of prayers. I popped it into the cassette player. The words he spoke were like healing salve to my emotions as I drove down the highway. By the time the tape had completed, my mood had been elevated into a tranquil state, and it relieved me as I calculated I had clipped off an hour of my journey as I drove down into Thermopolis. Driving through Wind River Canyon regardless of season was a scenic pleasure. It was always a relief to see Shoeshone lying out there in the horizon, as it was the halfway point. For as long as I could remember, this stop-off place was like the very end of somewhere.

I cruised through the small town, and headed to Casper. For the next two hours, I sang old hymns. There have been times in my life that it seemed as if Christ was sitting in the seat right next to me; this was one of those days. The melancholy mood had melted into a feeling of strength and peace, as the songs brought so many memories of a lifetime of experience.

Just a week before, I had received word that I had been awarded a year sabbatical to complete a qualitative research project. I was still so excited about the news, and it was going to be wonderful to have time to share my gratitude with friends who had been such a support through all the hard work of accomplishing the task of writing.

Much planning had gone into this week, as close friends I had grown up with, who also worked in Extension, would be attending the week-long training. We had arranged to have adjoining rooms at the motel. Each of us had stashed junk food into coolers. This had been the arrangement on previous trips, which had proved to be disastrous to anyone staying in the rooms adjacent to ours. We were the greatest of friends, and as the week would become tiresome, the evenings would grow in warmth and much laughter, as old stories were rehashed. I had always been blessed with an overactive sense of humor, so my retelling of past adventures would take on new and colorful dimensions. And of course, being the true-blue friends that they were, they would laugh at my antics.

By the time I had left Casper, it was the middle of the afternoon. The constant wind that customarily engulfs this area was unusually strong. Since the sun was still shining, I did not realize, as I drove along, that the temperature had plummeted.

As I looked back to the Medicine Bow Mountain range to the northeast, I saw dark volumes of seething, angry clouds coming down upon Shirley Basin. This was an area surrounded by a mountain that created its own climate. I had remembered my mother commenting in the past, "You don't want to get caught in Shirley Basin when a storm comes up."

Now, my mother was one of those homestead pioneers, who took on a form of bravery, not common to the modern-day woman. Her words had resonated in my storehouse of memory, and for that reason, if I had to drive through Shirley Basin in the winter; I was always relieved to see the sign, "Medicine Bow, 22 miles."

My Toyota Camry began to pull to the side of the road, and I quickly realized the wind had risen to gale proportions. I slowed down and gripped the steering wheel, trying to hold the car in my lane of traffic. Loneliness seemed to engulf my thoughts, which became a companion with those feelings of foreboding that had left home with me. I began to recite the 23rd Psalm over and over. I had just finished the last verse, "And I will live with you forever and forever and forever." Suddenly, I cried, "Dear God, send me more angels."

As I came down a hill, my car must have hit a patch of black ice, along with wind gusts, which caused the vehicle to begin a spin that went around and around in huge circles into the oncoming lane. Of course, there were no cars in sight, but as I spun around the second time, screaming the name of Jesus over and over, terror struck my heart as I saw, coming out of snow flurries, a huge snowplow coming directly towards me.

I was amazed, as I believed I was going to see God at that very moment. Thoughts passed so quickly, and there was an awareness of how close I felt His presence all through the day. It felt like a dark force had pushed me from behind right to the side of the huge plow. Then the darkness came.

Someone was banging on my window. I was gasping for air, as the blasts of wind were brutal on my face. I looked up to see a look of panic on the face of a man I did not know. The winter elements of wind and cold had caused deep wind-burned wrinkles, but he had a look of kindness. I would later feel sorry for the driver of the snowplow, as he thought I was dead. My car was on the side of the road, with a lone hubcap lying in the middle of the pavement. The snowplow was parked across the highway, the side of the bed smashed and the snow blade bent up into the air. I felt disoriented, and all I could think was for him to call my brother Wayne, who lived on a farm near Powell.

The highway patrolmen quickly arrived. He brought me a small quilt to wrap around my legs. It would take an hour for the ambulance to arrive. As I sat there, with most of the windows shattered, I realized the car was crunched in all around me. My seat was broken; glass was everywhere. I looked down and noticed my stomach had begun to swell. I lifted my shirt, and the entire front of me was purple. Panic seized me for a moment, as I knew I was hurt. Would I freeze or bleed to death out here, so far away from my family? Instantly as the thought came, I saw my son's face with such a depth of sorrow in his eyes.

My father's memory came to me so clear, as if he was right there in the car.

I took great strength from the last words my father spoke to me, before his death from the ravages of cancer: "I'll never give up hope; I'll never give up hope."

I quickly assessed my situation and came to the conclusion, "I am not dying today, I'm not cold, and I'm not going to cry. I am going to be thankful for that kind man over there sitting in the cab of the snowplow and the poor fellow out there having to wave the traffic around the debris my car left in the road."

I later was told the temperature had plummeted to more than twenty below. I just wanted to go home, but that was not going to happen, as the roads were closed behind me.

When the ambulance arrived, five volunteers had come to help. By this time, the sun had gone down, and the cold and wind currents had dropped again. The front passenger door had been shoved almost to the middle, so I was relieved they got the door open. A man got in and lifted me up out of my seat as the others managed to get me out from the driver's side. When the full impact of the wind blast hit me, I cried out, but then became immediately sick.

The gurney felt like stone and it was hard to lie back, and the last thing I wanted was to throw up, knowing I probably had some broken ribs. I kept requesting blankets, as I couldn't ever remember a time in my life I had been so cold. I was so grateful for the many people who helped me that night, but I had an ache in my heart, as I wanted my family.

How many times throughout my life have I discovered the caring of God in some of life's small details, which can mean a great deal? My UW Director, Glenn Whipple, came to the emergency room, which meant so much to me.

To my amazement, the local pastor of the Assembly of God, who just happened to be my childhood Sunday school teacher, Dave Garrett, and his wife Jean came and stood by my bed until I had stabilized. I noticed that Dave's arm was in a sling. He had just come through a horrific car accident himself. I knew he was in a great deal of pain, but it was such a relief to me that they had come.

That cold February day seems but a memory to me now. There is one thing everyone who comes so close to death can agree on: You are forever changed as you realize you have been given more time on this earth. From my time as a very young child growing up out on the northern plains of Wyoming, I had an awareness of God as my loving Heavenly Father and Great Shepherd. Is it any wonder that the stories of me as a little shepherd girl would surface and would come to me with such intensity that I would have to pen them to these pages? I knew the voice of the Shepherd, and I could trust him, as he gave me the courage that day out in Shirley Basin. I invite you to come with me now, as I share with you my experiences of life walking with this wonderful Shepherd of humanity.

After the cold winter day out in Shirley Basin, I was warm again, and life went on, but it was never the same. I slowly recovered, worked hard during my sabbatical year, and spent another year with the University of Wyoming. My eldest was a son by the name of Craig. For many years, he wanted me to come back to Michigan, not just for visits, but to live. Finally one day, in the early morning watching the sunrise, I knew I needed to be near those grandchildren, telling them lamby stories, and investing in them on a regular basis. The decision was not easily made, but much soul searching went into this process.

Teddy and Ronnie Jones came alongside me in the moving process, which always seems to be more difficult than we want to acknowledge. We drove across Interstate 80, with an auto transport in tow. I sat in the front with Ronnie with my little Yorkie dog Timmy. Teddy sat in the back seat, holding onto their sheep dog with a heavy hand. He was a very smart dog, but he made me nervous, as the look in his eye suggested he had thoughts of the tasty morsel sitting in the front with shaggy ears.

Craig, Sandy his wife, my daughter Rachel, her husband Mitch, and all the grandchildren met us with open arms that cool and crisp day in late October. I was hoping there would still be some golden, vibrant red leaves holding on for my friends from Wyoming. So it was with great delight, as we came around the south edge of Lake Michigan, my Wyoming friends were greeted with smashing bright crimson leaves. Life is a tradeoff. Wyoming has the rugged mountains that will always be a part of me. And then we have Michigan, with its lush foliage with so many types of trees and lakes, I will never acquire all their proper names.

CHAPTER 14

THE SILENT LESSONS FROM MY GARDEN

Who would think that mowing the lawn for the first time in the spring could bring such pleasure, but for some of us it does. My lawn was one of the last ones on the street to be mowed. It had been a long cold winter in Michigan. Spring did not come this year. Winter has passed directly into summer as the temperature today will be in the eighties.   The brutal winter took a toll on my lungs, already challenged by several bouts of pneumonia. For those of us who have had an extended time of sickness, we know the importance of taking hope in something to ward off melancholy and depression.

One of the simple pleasures in my life is the excitement of those first spring flowers. Last year, although my meager budget did not have a place for tulip bulbs, I bought them anyway. I went to the local hardware store, looked for a grandpa type and told him my plan for warding off the squirrels and deer. I came home with a wire mesh and wire cutters. The afternoon I planted my flowers was cold and wet. I hurried around the garden, trying to avoid cutting my hands, but exhilarated at the prospects of what awaited in the spring.

Even with all my planning the squirrels dug up about half of the bulbs, but I still had the loveliest yard full of fuchsia and soft pink feathery tulips. The variety that swept me away with joy was called Queen of Night. The elegant flowers were such a deep purple they appeared black from a distance.

How many times last spring did I find myself out in my yard as the sun was just coming up taking in the beauty before me? With a hot cup of coffee in hand and my Yorky type at my heels placing his paws carefully down into the grass filled with morning dew, I felt the presence of God. It was if his holiness would settle over me in that quiet place as a canopy.

Most of us think about time in units of years, months and days. I find myself more and more thinking about life as a moment in time as it quickly passes and then is gone.

This morning as I looked through my collection of pictures from last spring, I felt such disappoint that I didn't take pictures of the tulips. Last fall I wasn't that concerned, as I knew I would see those same colors again.

I took the plunge and bought another box of tulip bulbs in pastel shades. As I sit here on the deck looking out into the garden I am coming to the realization that those first tulips with shades of purple and fuchsia are now a moment in time that has past.

This winter after Christmas, I became ill. Day after day, I seemed to get worse instead of better. My lungs hurt so badly, I began to wonder what was really wrong with me. But then I would find myself thinking about all those wonderful tulips that would greet me in the spring and that simple pleasure would give me hope.

Those long days of illness were frustrating, as I had a book upstairs in my office that needed to be finished. Finally, I gained enough strength to begin writing again. As I looked at my dwindling savings, I knew in my heart if I didn't finish the Homestead book this spring, it would never get done. I prayed day after day for strength and that passion to return that allows me to write like the wind.

Then one day in late February I began to write again. The stories began to form in my mind in the night hours and as I took my shower in the mornings. My office chair had broken, so I sat hour after hour on a folding chair, until I could no longer type. All those years of research, now in thick binders, was sprawled out in the guest bedroom. A hard copy of each of the chapters was neatly placed in order on the table next to my desk. I had sticky notes on the wall. I was on the home stretch. It seemed as if every fiber within me was set on that last chapter being completed.

I had pushed myself, but that was not unusual for me, as I have always been challenged by working hard. One morning I woke up with a stiff neck.

I thought I had just slept wrong and it would pass, but the pain didn't go away. A few days later my daughters would be with me in the emergency room and life would never be the same.

The heavy medication caused dizziness and extreme fatigue. I was unsteady on my feet, so I walked with a cane. The doctor told me my short term memory would return in a few months, but that was very frustrating to me as I found it hard to think clearly.

Every morning I prayed for patience and for a grateful heart as my family and friends had shown me so much kindness. The details and severity of my sickness will wait for another time.

Michigan has finally had a few days of warmth. How many times this winter have I drawn courage from the expectation of those multicolored tulips that would greet me in the spring? Countless times I would say. But alas, as loved ones would help me, as I was so unsteady on my feet, I would inspect my flower beds. Even with all the care that went into the planting the deer ate the tops of the buds and squirrels managed dig up the bulbs.

This Monday, I looked out on my lawn, so badly needing to be mowed. I saw where the deer had bedded down under the evergreen in the front yard. I seemed to have a burst of energy but was still unsteady on my feet. I went over and asked my neighbor ladies to watch out for me. I managed to get my lawn mower started. It was a challenge, but oh what a wonderful feeling to hold onto the handle bars and get around my yard.

It is hard to express how I felt, as I made my way around the back yard. I couldn't see very many tulips, and those left were only stubs except for one group at the back side of the garage of the new pastels I had planted last fall.

I finally had to face the fact that all the fuchsia and deep purple tulips had been eaten.

Each time I made a circle around the yard, I looked at those tulips at the back side of the garage. How had they survived the deer? My artist eyes give me a keen sense of color. I expend a great deal of time in picking out the colors for a quilt or in the color palette I choose each spring for my garden so that every color enhances and blends to bring harmony. The delicate pink didn't seem to blend with the deep orange and red. That evening as I sat on my deck with my Yorky type dog Timmy the only color, except green in my backyard, was that small patch of tulips at the back fence. I could see the paint peeling on the garage paneling. I would not have the strength for that repair this summer.

Not only have I found this backyard to become my muse, but the old house as well has been my quiet place to write. The grain of the wood in the oak French doors is beautiful to me. The large dining room full of windows, filled with the fragrance of croissant rolls that have greeted my family and friends have been a source of joy to me. On and on I could describe this place that has been my home. But now in this season of my life, the flights of stairs have become a great burden. The expense of keeping up this big old house is no longer possible.

And now I find myself back out on the deck in the warm evening with Timmy snuggled on my lap. We both are looking at the back yard. He is looking for squirrels. My eyes are fixed on the small group of tulips near the back of the garage.

If the expanse of my yard had been full of tulips as my dreams had anticipated all winter, my intense gaze would not have been focused on that small group of tulips that had survived the winter's plunder.

There are those moments in time that have a way of speaking into that inner part of the soul if we will pay attention. As I looked out on the colors displayed so beautifully in the tulip bed, I began to think: "That is me." The soft pink and white petals are that part of me that can see life through a delicate gentle gaze not everyone understands. The lemon yellow describes my all-encompassing love of beauty and life and the smile on a small child's face. And alas, the mix of vibrant deep red and yellow combined are just the perfect colors that speak so clearly to me in this time of testing. The overwhelming physical pain mixed with confusion and everything in life taking a 180 degree turn leaves me holding onto faith as I have done so many times throughout my life. But this time is different. I already am experiencing a depth of compassion within myself for others, as I have never in my whole life felt so helpless and needing the loving care of others. Part of me wants to fight this, but a greater sense tells me to just be quiet and concentrate on the beauty of that small garden growing at the back side of the garage. I checked the weather this morning and I do believe summer is almost here, as it will be in the eighties. It is already getting very warm as I drink my coffee early this morning, praying quietly and looking out in the backyard. I look out to my flower bed. "What am I seeing?" Timmy and I take a stroll out there and sure enough back behind the other brilliant colors are a few deep purple tulips beginning to bloom and over to the side is a delicate pink flower standing by itself.

What a wonderful gift you are to me little group of tulips with all your wonderful colors. I don't have answers for my physical health at this time. Day by day I become stronger and one day very soon the last chapter of my homestead book will be complete. Somehow, I know as I tell of the courageous families in our small community in Wyoming back after the war, there will be another tapestry of colors woven into the telling.

How will I have the courage to say goodbye to this old home and garden? All I can say is when that time comes, the Heavenly Shepherd I have known so well, down through the years will be close by and it will be well with my soul and my heart will be ready for that next sunrise that always comes in every season of life. AMEN

Written on May 12, 2011, Patricia Booher

CHAPTER 15

EMPTY FLOWER POTS

This assortment of flower pots has been collected in the last few years. The large terra cotta pot looks ancient as the deep hues of sage green moss quietly seep up through the crusted orange texture giving it a look of the old country. The teal strawberry pot was picked out by my granddaughters. And on and on I could go narrating a story of each little pot setting on my deck this morning.

My budget has been limited, so I only felt I dare add one maybe two to the collection each summer. So now after a few years in Michigan, I have a number of contrasting sizes and shapes.

By this time of the season, all these flower pots would be full of wonderful hues of fuchsia, purple, lemon yellow, periwinkle blue and just a touch of snowy white; but not this year. So without the floral arrangements I find myself looking intently at these empty flower pots before me this morning.

My first assortment of flower pots began while living in Shell, Wyoming. There were four picture windows on the north and west view of the house. The builder had been careful in planning a panoramic scene of the Big Horn Mountain range for as far as the eye could see. It was nothing short of spectacular for me and all those guests who sat with me out on the deck on summer evenings.

Although my job with the university required a good deal of travel my affection for arrangements of flowers on the deck grew with intensity from year to year. This would not have been possible if my neighbor and friend Linda had not been willing to water those flowers everyday when I was away working, as the hot summer days were very intense up next to the mountain range.

Each year I would add to my collection of flower pots, with the wooden containers always my favorite along with the expanded varieties and colors of flowers which would be displayed in front of every window.

I put a great deal of thought into how I blended the colors and often after sitting for a while, would find myself digging up roots to move to another flower pot. My job was demanding, so the flowers actually became my muse in the evenings. It was hard to part with the flower pots, but it was also gratifying to give them to Linda when I moved.

I fondly remember several years later going to see Linda and KL. There was the terra cotta pot decorated with impressions of grapevines sitting on her front step.

And now once again I find myself in my own personal journey in a state of flux and transition. I managed to get through the waiting period with the biopsy procedure on the horizon. Because of how one can be filled with fear of the unknown, I had managed to "buck-up" in my attitude and feelings before that morning. That is a term I often use, when I just need to head into the wind, as life's challenges come to all of us, don't they.

Because the mass is deeply imbedded in my neck, it was difficult to obtain a sample, so the procedure was repeated several times. I lay very quietly squeezing a rubber ball, but by the time I was able to be finished I felt drained and a bit overwhelmed. The next few days I was very quiet and exhausted, so house work and other chores were laid aside.

One of my favorite places is sitting with my Yorky type dog Timmy just under the canopy of the old maple tree hanging over my deck in the cool of early mornings. Thus I found myself setting comfortably on my chartreuse colored cushion with Timmy watching my every move from the adjacent deck chair, also lined with the same cushion. Actually he would prefer to be sunning himself on the deck as he likes to silently sneak off looking for squirrels. The thought of him running across the street in hot pursuit is something that is not even possible to consider at this point. He is my little writing buddy. There are times I almost wonder if he understands what I am saying to him.

Now let us go back and look at those empty flower pots once again. I have not only acquired flower pots, but an array of different sizes of shepherd's hooks and circular stands to give height and depth to my arrangements.

Years ago I was privileged to sit under the teaching of some of the most famous and talented instructors in the art of embellishment. I gained an appreciation of using texture and color to enhance clothing design. This eye for style and design has been carried out to my backyard gardens and deck containers filled with flowers.

I always knew I had a flare for dress designing, but I never saw myself as a writer until one of those times, such as now, I found myself in a state of flux and transition. I had come through back surgery. The pain in recovery seemed at times unbearable. One day I was quietly sitting and looking out of my picture window observing the mountain scene in a snowstorm that had lasted for days. That silent voice, oh I know so well, from a life time of loving God, spoke inside of me, "Go find a writing journal and write!" And so I did.

That was many years ago. The beauty that came out of writing down in words what I saw with my eyes and spirit has been a challenge to see more keenly the world around me. For example, this morning I am writing about those empty flower pots on my deck. As I look up from the computer screen my gaze takes me over to myneighbor's backyard. A small sparrow is perched on the edge of the feeder along with a squirrel upside down getting his fill and spilling bird seed all over the ground. But then the squirrel jumps down on the ground and retrieves what he has spilt, so I guess things have a way of working out, don't they.

Somehow, I just seem to know that this last Mother's Day will be a special memory for me. Craig's family had invited me to go with them to their favorite restaurant in downtown Ann Arbor on Sunday afternoon. I appreciated being invited, but felt unsure of myself, as I was still dealing with a great deal of fatigue and confusion. Eating was difficult as I choked very easily, on that day I was very quiet and just listened to my family visiting. As we left the restaurant, Craig came along side of me and I held on to his strong arm. I didn't want him to know how relieved I felt at that moment, as I didn't want him to worry, but I was so unsteady on my feet. As we walked to the car we saw a lovely flower nursery over on a side street, so off we went. As I waited for the family I sat out on the sidewalk on a wicker couch with Craig. I looked over to the side and saw a gardenia plant. It took me a few moments to remember the name of the plant, as my short term memory had been so challenged, but then finally with relief it came to me. "Oh Craig, it is my most favorite flower in the entire world." Andthen I quickly dropped the subject, as I knew without even looking it was very expensive.

Weeks went by and slowly I became stronger so I began to collect my beautiful flower pots from the garage and set them on the deck. I couldn't seem to get that gardenia out of my mind. One morning, as I had my morning time reading the Bible I came across a scripture that means a great deal to me.

"Let not your heart be troubled; you believe in God,
believe also in Me.
"In My father's house are many mansions; if it were not so, I
would have told you. I go to prepare a place for you.

"And if I go and prepare a place for you, I will come again and receive you to Myself; that where I am, there you may be also."
John 14:1-3 NKJV

For most of us, we seem to have this idea that life goes on forever. That is until we are faced with the possibility that this is not always true. As I pondered the verse that morning, I once again thought about the fragrance of my favorite flower and thought of how God, the great creator knows each of us so well. I do believe that one day when I am in Heaven I will see about me the beautiful gardenia I have loved so well from my youth.

The day finally came for the doctor's appointment when I would know the results of my biopsy. My daughters were anxious for me, but I just seemed to have a sense that I needed to drive myself to U of M hospital. I was surprised when I arrived an hour early. I didn't want to sit in the waiting room for such a long time so I decided to drive down the street and maybe get a cup of coffee. About half a mile down the street I saw a Kroger grocery store. I thought, "Well I need to stop and get some tomatoes, so I will just get them now."

I had already vowed that I would not tempt myself this spring as I knew buying flowers was not in my budget, for sure. There were no trips to garden nurseries in my horizon. I pulled into the parking lot, and you guessed it, right out in front of the store was a tent with an assortment of plants and flowers. All self control left me as I found myself under the shade of the awning. I looked down in front of me and just had to catch my breath. It just can't be? I always look for these flowers but even in the most exclusive nurseries, I feel fortunate to find them and now I see a whole row of beautiful gardenia plants loaded with buds just waiting to bloom.

I was almost afraid to ask the attendant how much the plants cost. When he told me I just couldn't believe it. I stood there for a few moments as the heaviness of the morning lifted off of me. I knew I didn't dare start crying, but carefully went back and forth until I found just the perfect one for me. After I paid the gentleman, I said, "I just want to thank you, I am on my way to get the results of my biopsy, and I have been so sad this morning. The gardenia is my most cherished flower in the entire world, so I bless you that you were here for me." He looked at me with such kindness, "Oh, I wish the best for you. May I carry your plant to the car for you?"

After he had placed the plant in the back seat, I reached out and shook his hand. "Thank you, thank you sir; I think I have the courage I need now." Such a look of compassion I saw in that elderly Asian gentleman that morning.

I like to call them "God Encounters." In our busy lives, we often fail to take note of those personal touches of God's grace in our lives. In my own journey with this Shepherd of Heaven, I have found him to be very much interested in the affairs of mankind. He knows each of us in the smallest details of our lives. He is always near coming along to give each of us the faith and courage for every circumstance, if only we allow him to.

I am thinking this morning of the story in the Bible of the ten lepers. Jesus was passing through a small village on his way to Jerusalem. He was met by ten lepers who stood far off from everyone else as the disease was contagious. The physical and emotional suffering of the poor souls with this horrible disfiguring disease is hard to imagine.

They were the outcasts of society. Just the kind of people, the compassion of this Savior from heaven would be touched with. When Jesus saw them he said, "Go, show yourselves to the priests."
Luke 17:11 - 19

What I find interesting in this story of healing, is that only one man returned to thank Jesus for his healing. Where were the other nine? I believe we could draw a parallel from this story. How many times, in our own lives are we touched by the Master of the Universe? How often do we hear him speak in that silent voice in the midnight hours? "Be still and at peace, I will never leave you nor forsake you." Only if we listen, can we hear his voice, but that does not mean he isn't nearby.

How many times in my own life, has it appeared that my flower pots were empty? If I took time to quietly sit in the presence of the Lord of my life, he would come and fill those empty and barren places with a thing of beauty. Not only would I feel the blessings fromHeaven, but my own insight and compassion of those less fortunate then myself would come into view.

As I drove to my doctor's appointment that morning, my heart was so grateful for the beautiful plant full of blooms in my back seat. The kindness of the man who spoke with me only added to the tenderness of that experience I drove around the parking lot looking for a shade tree. Although it was still cool that morning, I wanted nothing to happen to my new found treasure. I rolled all the windows down just a bit and prayed that guardian angels would protect my car.I walked with a spring in my step, knowing that whatever lay beforeme I would have the faith and courage I needed.

Regardless of the outcome, another layer of God's character was forming in those hidden parts of my soul and spirit. I do believe one of the greatest components of a rich life is just learning to be thankful, not always in the big stuff, but even in the smallest of things, taking the time to be gracious and just say, "Thank you." All I can say at this point is:

"Oh precious Lord and Father, I thank you for the empty flower pots of my own life. I know so well that you have a way of making beauty out of ashes, the colors of a rainbow more beautiful after a storm and the gardenia planted now in my teal colored flower pot, more cherished then anything I could imagine.

AMEN
Patricia Booher, June 6, 2011

CHAPTER 16

THE BLIGHTED PETALS OF LIFE

For those of us Michigan dwellers, we have an ability to enjoy the beautiful and perfect weather of late August because we know what is just around the corner. This last winter was long and brutal. I well remember by late February it becomes apparent that it is hard to endure one more day of the chill, and then we are blessed with spring. The leaves ever so slowly begin to appear and we all sigh with relief. We have made it through another winter. Summer comes with the great expectation of Michigan cherries.

We have a few weeks when going to Lake Michigan is just awesome and then the humid oppressing heat along with mosquitoes causes us to hide indoors, not that we nature lovers want that. As we get older we find the heat can become a dangerous factor leaving us exhausted and off kilter but we know fall is just around the corner.

This morning I put on my winter robe as I descended the stairs to let an eager little Yorky out for his business. I fixed that dark cup of coffee, chose a beautiful mug out of my stash and made my way into my sunroom for morning prayers. After a while I decided to sit out on the deck and have breakfast. As I finished eating I turned my chair around to face the flowers out in my quiet haven of a backyard.

I glanced over and looked at my gardenia plant that has brought me such pleasure this summer and there I found another blossom. I stepped over, leaned down and smelled the fragrance, almost unearthly.

I sat back down as the memories came back of so many other days this year. In a way it seems as if it was a dream, except on this day another mountain appears in the horizon.

The sickness, beginning right after Christmas, required more faith then I thought was in me. But with each new level of seriousness, the faith beyond measure beyond my own capacity would be there.

As I sat there looking at the gardenia blossom, memories of the night began to surface. Those pre-dawn dreams came to me. That voice from Heaven, oh I know so well, was speaking. "I am giving you a new layer of courage. Head into the wind just as you have chosen to do throughout your journey. This storm will be greater than the past, but in your time of affliction, I have been strengthening your fiber and I am coming to give you direction."

I drew closer to the flower in front of me. As I studied the petals, I noticed the one at the top had been damaged. I was going to take a picture, but then decided the flower was not perfect.

Nature speaks to us if we will only listen. How many times in scripture do we read of how God takes those scorched places in humanity and makes himself real? I do believe it is built into mankind to have that will to just "Do it myself." For some it is even hard to give anyone else credit when great tasks are accomplished, and what a hard thing it is for some to have the ability to say "Thank you."

It is only natural to acknowledge the most brilliant and clever person. Why would anyone favor a beggar over a rich man? Wouldn't' we all rather walk down the street with that handsome or beautiful specimen of human kind, rather than choose that one weary and barely able to walk.

I have in my mind the memory of a mother from long ago now. Our first born, Craig was about two years old. Dare I say he was a beautiful child, so brilliant, a head full of blond curly locks and personality that could charm anyone. Truly he was the joy of my life.

One afternoon we went to a local amusement park. My husband took Craig up on the Ferris wheel. I never have enjoyed heights. As I watched them go round and round, hearing the squeals and laughter of our small child, my gaze fell upon another father with his young son. No squeals and laughter came from this child. I'm not sure he was even aware of his surroundings. I looked on that child with great pity, wondering how I would feel if he were my child. And yet as I looked at the father's face, I saw strength and great love for his child.

What brought great sorrow to my heart is when my gaze came back to earth and I looked over to the side, I saw the mother. She was watching me with an intense gaze, reading my thoughts. It was just in the flicker of the moment, but I saw into the soul of that mother. "What does this stranger see in my child, would she accept him or turn him away just as so many others have done." What can one do in a situation like this? To say anything to that precious mother would have only made it worse for her.

As I sat there this morning studying the petals on that little flower with the blighted petal, I saw new beauty. I ran upstairs and grabbed my little digital camera wanting to catch the morning sun before it made its way up over the roof tops. How many times in my own life have I seen those broken and bruised places? Those wounded and parched crevices of my soul, without God's healing touch would never be mended. And yet today, I find it so true that in my greatest weakness, the Shepherd of Heaven, Jesus Christ comes and brings his strength.

And He said to me, "My grace is sufficient for you,
for My strength is made perfect in weakness."
Therefore most gladly I will rather boast in my infirmities,
that the power of Christ may rest upon me.
Therefore I take pleasure in infirmities, in reproaches, in needs,
in persecutions, in distresses, for Christ's sake.
For when I am weak, then I am strong.
II Corinthians 12:9 – 10 NKJV

I am not asking for the hard and the difficult, in fact if there were a way I could walk away from this circumstance I find myself in at this moment, what a relief it would be. If I didn't know, without a doubt, that the Lord leads my every step, that he sees every tear caressing my cheek, that he hears every weary cry unto him, then I would be in the depths of despair.

The sparrows have been fluttering all about me in the last few days. They bring to my remembrance the mention of how the Lord cares even for the little birds of the air.

Sometimes it is hard to make sense out of life. One thing is for sure, along this journey, if you and I listen, if we quietly see the damaged petal of a flower, if we hear the pulse of humanity through the eyes of God, then we know he does all things well. He takes those dry and parched places of life, and makes a garden of praise. He takes the sorrow and turns it into joy.

All that is required of you and me is to come to that place of reverence and awe of a God who planned this entire universe. When the journey of man takes him to that place he is willing to lay everything at the feet of Jesus and be humbled by the presence of a Holy God, then that blighted and wounded place becomes the very thing that causes the shackles to fall off of blinded eyes.

The beauty in this experience is that life takes on insight as to the suffering of another. As we look about we see those who have made the choice to take the experience of pain that has been healed by God's grace and pour the fragrance of healing onto another soul wounded by life's heart aches.

"The Spirit of the Lord is upon Me,
Because He has anointed Me

To preach the gospel to the poor;
He has sent Me to heal the brokenhearted,
To proclaim liberty to the captives
And recovery of sight to the blind,
To set at liberty those who are oppressed;
To proclaim the acceptable year of the Lord."
Luke 4:18 – 19 NKJV

One day very soon, we will look into the face of our redeemer and Savior and we will know as we are known. There will be no blighted petals, but in his presence, our garments will be as white as snow. We will be filled with the radiance of God's glory. All tears will be washed away and we will forever be in the presence of our Savior,

Jesus Christ.

CHAPTER 17

CUPS OF PRAYER

It seems I can almost see the finish line on this book on grief. I would say I am past the middle mark of the climber to the top of the mountain. I have come to recognize in the initial stages of writing that the outline and chapters seem to shift in place as the story unfolds.

I am grateful that from the very beginning of my "life of writing" on that cold winter day back in 1994, recovering from back surgery, I had the wisdom to date each poem written.

For now after so many years, I can go back and recollect the time, place and situation where I found myself.

After months of recovering from the concussion, I was able to write snippets of this journey of my own life. I thought at the time the "Cups of Prayer," would be the last chapter of this grief book. But then the experience of the "Cotton Balls in the Sky," gave me such a boost in faith and courage that it became the ending. So you might ask, "Why have you now placed, "Cups of Prayer," on the other side of the middle of the story?" This decision was made in the midnight hours last night as I pondered how this beautiful experience we call prayer has really impacted my entire life.

I would explain prayer as a plumb line which is described as a string with a weight on the end running vertically that is used in building to make sure the structure is centered. As you read this chapter, you might be thinking, "but I have never been one who prays." I want to encourage you that as you pray if you have a true and sincere heart, God hears you. It might be a simple prayer like I describe as paper cup prayers, or a prayer in travail for a nation gone astray or a loved one dying from cancer. Yes, I have come to understand prayer is that direct vertical line from humanity here on the earth to our Heavenly Father.

Last night as I sat here looking at the picture, the memories rolled back to that night sitting with my mother. That was a sad time for me, as I knew that soon I would be leaving that home in Shell I had grown to love so well. I was now into the middle of the year's sabbatical which had begun in July.

It was a great disappointment as I had such a sense of urgency to get the research done, and then the car wreck happened. There really is no adequate way to describe what had happened that night out in Shirley Basin as after the first impact I was unconscious. Writing has becomes a creative outlet for me especially when I am going through a great trial such as trying to recover my health in those years.

I knew I would be selling the home in Shell, so I had already had a moving sale when she came that December evening. I don't know what I had prepared for dinner; I just remember I was so happy she was with me that evening. I had sold the dining room set, so that evening the meal was served on a card table. After we ate, she quietly listened as I read a few of the snippets of stories of my life as faith was developing to a new and deeper level of experience.

Before I began reading, "Cups of Prayer," I placed the five cups on the table and picked up each one as I described the prayer it related to. I must say I was not able to read this snippet without crying. The picture was taken much later in my vintage home in Michigan. It was a beautiful summer day as I arranged each of my much loved cups before me with my clay pots filled with flowers all around.

CUPS OF PRAYER

A number of years ago I was with a group of about eighty members of a church choir taking a concert tour across Germany and Spain. The schedule that had been planned for us was not very realistic for that large a group.

Each day began early with a long journey, and then in the evening we would have a concert in a new city.

There were days when stopping for a meal was not possible. In our American culture, this is not a problem, as even in small towns one can find a fast food restaurant that quickly prepares and packages food to be eaten on the run. Not so in the highways and byways we traversed. There were no such restaurants where paper cups and plates were used. The two bus drivers openly showed their disgust at the American custom of eating on the bus. This was surprising to me, thinking that this American custom was observed everywhere else.

Many years have passed since the choir trip, and I find myself thinking about those times and seasons of my life and the containers that were used to drink out of. This morning I went through my cupboards and pulled out cups I use in this season of my life.

I have placed the collection in front of me as I write. The first cup I am looking at is Styrofoam. This cup is a familiar part of our culture. In the fast pace life so many of us find ourselves, we would be hard hit if we did not have a good stock of these cups to use. Many restaurants would not be able to serve a meal if their supply of paper products ran out. Some families have opted to use paper cups and plates for every day meals for convenience.

If I were to classify the cups setting in front of me today, the Styrofoam would come in last as far as preference. The fact is sometimes, I need to use paper cups. As I liken this cup to the prayers, I have prayed throughout my life, I am most grateful for those paper cup prayers. When I was a young child, I prayed a simple prayer to ask Jesus Christ to come into my life. It was sincere, not very profound. But it was words that came out of my heart to a Savior that I was just meeting.

During those early days of my walk with Christ, his love was poured into my little cup. Everything was so new to me, and I was so full of joy in realizing that God's spirit was down inside my heart.

As a young girl, I became aware that my little paper cup could be caught in the wind and blown over. Because the drink of life was so precious, I didn't want to spill it or let it be poured out on the ground, so I would hold it in my hands.

As I rode my horse across those hills filled with the spring smell of sagebrush, under the protection of Heart Mountain, the beloved place of childhood, I prayed. I didn't want my words to be lost in the vast universe, so I began to keep my prayers in an old metal cup.

We used this cup on family fishing trips. It was a bit scuffed, dented, and the metal showed through the blue coating, but as I drank hot chocolate, my little cup brought comfort to me.

I loved my family deeply but even as a young child, as I look back now, I recognize there were times I felt great loneliness and melancholy which I now understand as a writer that would one day come on the scene. Often times I would seek out places of solitude to pray those childlike prayers. I am sure that is why God, my Heavenly Father, became a very close friend and confidant in those growing up years.

I grew up and had my own family. I loved to hear the laughter of my children, loved to see their excitement on discovering the beauty of life around them. In those busy years of life, home was the central focus. The old metal cup was no longer suitable, so I put it in the kitchen cupboard and took out a pottery cup, the color of ivory. It was a larger heavy cup that kept my coffee warm in the morning.

As my prayers ascended into the heavenlies, God poured into my cup strength for each day, wisdom, longsuffering, gentleness, and tender caring love. In those years I never lost my roots of childhood and awareness of God's love for me. The Wyoming sagebrush so delicately painted on my earthen cup intertwined all my family and friends who encircled my life in those years.

The river of my life has taken some turns and twists that I had not planned. Some winter storms have caused floods that have washed away the moss covered river banks and rugged boulders have been uncovered that have brought much pain. But in the torrential rains, I never forgot to pray. In fact in those years the oil of God's Holy Spirit was poured over my prayers, so that they became a sweet fragrance that ascended into the heavens.

Many years have passed since those first simple prayers of salvation. Each day in the times of quiet meditation and solace I feel the richness of God' presence. It is time to add another cup to my collection.

I am a lover of the simple elegance of life. One of my greatest pleasures in the morning is to drink coffee or tea out of a beautiful china cup. So, today as I write about my cups of prayer, I have chosen a delicate cup made of bone china. It is a regal cup setting on little pedestals. The handle has the touch of an artist's eye, with the delicate engravings of roses, the flower that always brings a breath of beauty into my heart.

As I look back over my past there is a deep sadness because as a young child this is the cup that I wanted to portray my life, but alas as I have seen the seasons of my journey unravel into today's realities, I have to choose another cup. It too is a china cup, but it has a lid.

In this season of my life, some of my prayers are in earshot of others, but the prayers that come from the very depths of my heart and soul, sometimes spoken with a broken and contrite spirit are in a desert place alone. This china cup lid holds in the heat in order for the flavor to be enriched. The tea and coffee drank from this cup have been steeped to such a degree that it brings a calmness to my whole being. As I hold the delicate shape of this cup, I realize how tenderly my Lord has cradled me in his hands all of my life. The artist's skill in painting the intricate rose petals, speaks to me of God's protection over my life. He has brought beauty out of ashes given me a love of life beyond my understanding.

As I lift the lid, I see a crack from the top of the brim, descending down to under the handle. "Oh Lord, please let me choose the other china cup. This cup has been marred by life's heartaches." As I sit in the quiet presence of my Master, tears begin to course down my face, as I look back over my life, but in the solitude and stillness I feel a gentle touch brushing away the tears, and a soft voice, I have grown to know to be my heavenly Father, "No cherished daughter, this is the cup I have chosen for you. Look my child I have healed the broken place. It is not a scar to lament, but it is likened to the scars in my hands I suffered for you. I felt your pain; I carried you when you no longer could stand. As you look at your china cup, you see how it has been marred, but others who love you will see the great miracle of healing that has been done. I will wipe away all your tears as you go out into a world of other travelers who have scars. You will bring a prayer of courage, a prayer of comfort, a healing balm of my spirit.

Walk on my daughter, holding your cup. I have many sunrises for you to see. I have many things to tell you, many dreams to fulfill in your life, many prayers to answer. Take your cup and pour out the oil of healing to humanity who are now in their own valley of sorrow."

Patricia McClaflin Booher, December 2001

SECTION IV:

LIGHT AT THE END OF THE TUNNEL

CHAPTER 18

THE SUN DID COME UP TODAY

As I pause to think about this last year of living, not only for our nation, but throughout the world one would think we have always lived with the fear of Covid 19. What was life like before this pandemic?

For my family we came together in the early part of December of the previous year to honor our mother. We spent the week before her funeral together planning the event which was very meaningful, not only for our family but for her friends of many years. She missed her 100th birthday by just thirty-seven days. I have missed her keenly but have been grateful she is in Heaven and did not have to live in isolation this past year.

I have mentioned already that during those first months of lock-down I was able to get the "Beloved Homeland," published. What a relief it is to see the book finally in print, but also such a disappointment my mother did not live to see this.

As I have listened day after day of the many elderly who died alone in nursing homes, my heart is deeply grieved, remembering how we were able to honor our mother.

My family was very protective of me from the beginning. I tried to be very careful as I am on the other side of the middle seventies and have had multiple battles with pneumonia. I regret that I did come down with Covid.

I had hoped when I first became ill I would be one of those who seemed to sail through Covid, but that was not going to be the outcome for me, as I became very ill for an extended period of time. I have heard it described as the thought process and short term memory is in a muddle and that is just the way it was. I could not think, did not dare let myself feel emotion or cry as I just could not breath. I won't go through all the symptoms I had, just to say I knew I was very ill and felt I had to survive this time.

Day after day, as I heard of the tragic family stories, I knew I needed to somehow gain the energy to begin the process of getting this grief book in print. At this time in my own journey as an author I do have a sense of what this entails. It has been my experience in the past that the story, regardless of the book title at some point seems to take on a life of its own.

I have shared throughout this story of grief how those past experiences of survival and overcoming grief and adversity have built within me a reserve of strength. I have decided to include these snippets of writings that came out of the silent time of the concussion several years ago. It is apparent as one reads through the Table of Contents in my own story, that those past life experiences were not wasted.

Those months of recovering from the concussion I describe as the silent time as I came to understand the vital need to be very quiet and not challenge my thought and creative process. Computer time became very limited. There was a time I did not have the energy or mental power to write, but then after a time when strength returned I would always be amazed at the stories of life that would unfold.

SPARROWS AND CROWS

When the blast of winter hits in early January here in Michigan, we seem to be caught off guard each time at how cold it really is. As we get older, it seems the cold is even more brutal and we find ourselves chuckling to see the young set walking around in shorts without a heavy coat.

I will give just a brief explanation for you the reader so you too will understand the significance for me as I heard sparrows singing in the winter season. It was the first weekend of December. As I went to bed that Saturday evening, I was very weary, but as I looked back on the week's activities, I was happy that I had been able to enjoy time with several dear friends and also spend the day with my grandson Luke at his Bible Quiz contest. We had to drive a long way that day, and I had been busy during the contest keeping score.

I am guilty of forgetting or not taking the time to drink enough water. For whatever reason, in the night I became very sick and passed out hitting my head on the bathtub. I was in such a weakened state I had a hard time finding my way back to bed, only to wake up again on the floor, cold, not knowing where I was for a few minutes. It took hours to manage to get to my phone in the next room so I could call my daughter. The next day I vomited for several hours and still did not realize I had a concussion until later. Looking back on the next few weeks, I am glad I did not realize recovery would be such a challenge. It is seven weeks since that night and my brain energy is still healing slowly, along with fatigue.

I am a writer and a researcher so reading and computer work are a big part of my everyday life.

I am now able to read a few pages a day and for that I am grateful. In those days of recovery when the temperature was sub-zero and ice covered the ground, I knew I was not safe taking my little dog Bezoo out to the end of the drive near the big round bushes, although that is where he always wants to go. But on this morning the temperatures hovered around 12 degrees so it felt like a blast of warmth. The sun was shining, not a cloud in the sky, so my emotions were lifted as it had been many difficult days of confusion and complete exhaustion. In the distance, I could hear the happy chirping of sparrows.

Oh my goodness, there must have been hundreds of little birds filling the branches with their happy songs. As we approached they immediately became silent but as we moved closer and stood there they slowly began to chirp again.

I felt an overwhelming presence of God's glory that morning as I quietly stood looking at those little birds so fat and healthy with their happy songs of life. This has been a time of testing my faith for sure, but then I have been in holding patterns throughout my life, not knowing what the future would hold for me.

This time is different, as I have never before had a brain injury, so I am surprised at how delicate my thought process is now. It is difficult to visit, because I find sometimes I cannot complete sentences, but this time will pass. I have a sense that the spiritual depth and growth in this last month has been under the surface of conscious reasoning, but now I am slowly having those thoughts.

The only way I can put it into words is that at times I feel I have one foot on the threshold of Heaven.

I then come back to a world that so desperately needs this insight of Gods' love for all of his creation. After a few moments Bezoo and I slowly walked back to my apartment. The trees to the south have been removed, much to my disappointment. Last summer as those huge tractors came into the forest I liked to call my own; I would make my trek down to the working men and see that the trees had been sitting in a large swamp. Now it is barren with only the swamp in view, but there are a few remaining trunks with barren branches sticking up in random spots.

The chirping of the little sparrows has been refreshing, but now I hear loud and obtrusive squawking from what sounded like crows. Now I do understand that we are all God's creatures and I want to also appreciate Mr. Crow. But on this morning the air and sunshine were such a blessing as I enjoyed the happy sparrows.

Every man and woman born on this earth was in God's mind before we were in the womb. He has promised that he would never leave us or forsake us. Each person has a choice in living out this journey, for some hard and for others not such a challenge. But I do believe in every season, regardless of the circumstance that deep underlying faith and trust that God does all things well helps us in those quiet times of recovery. Looking back on this time of hiding away in the quiet place, I am in awe of those thoughts that are coming now of this God of Heaven who far surpasses man's human reason.

He has shown you, O mortal, what is good. And what does the LORD require of you? To act justly and to love mercy and to walk humbly with your God. Micah 6:8NIV

January 18, 2018

I am thinking of so many others who, just like myself, are having the residual effects of a heavy dose of Covid. Each week as I look back on my own recovery, I am grateful and yet it is so easy to overdue. I explain it this way, "One step forward, three steps back." That happens on those days when I am not using wisdom. In this time of writing I want to just keep going, but I have learned the hard way that I have to pay close attention. This next snippet of my life was during the recovery time of concussion and because of that experience I knew in these last few months in the silent time, something beautiful would come out of it and now I am seeing the sunsets over the lake and my heart is blessed.

SUNRISE IN WINTER

As you look at this picture, you might be wondering why I would have chosen this one to be in this story. Read down a few lines and it will be evidence of how it so accurately describes how I was in the process of overcoming the concussion. It was not going to be a quick fix. I am grateful now that even in those months when writing was very difficult for me, I had been able to pen my thoughts and date each addition of story line.

Through-out these snippets of stories I have shared with you, I have woven present with past and then looking with hope to the future with hope that I will come out of this time with even a stronger faith and purpose then before these months of sickness. I will roll back several years and bring you along with me on my own journey of how my faith and courage had grown even though it was a long process of healing.

I remember when I was a young girl growing up out there on those windswept plains of northern Wyoming, the winter mornings were cold. One would want to crawl down deep under the covers for warmth, but for our family we would be up early taking care of livestock before the school bus arrived. Although it was early morning, our father would be up drinking coffee watching the sunrise if there wasn't a snow storm covering the sky.

I knew he very likely had already been out in the barns checking on the sheep flocks and other livestock. He used to tell me how much he enjoyed the quiet of the mornings as he would gather his thoughts for the day. Well, sadly he has been away from us now for many years, although we take comfort as we know he is in Heaven.

How I have wished so many times in my own later years that I would have just stolen away out of the comfort of my warm bed and gone in and sat with this man so full of the horse sense of life.

How ironic that in this season of my own life, as the hair has turned to grey, I find myself getting up way before the eastern sky shows a glimmer of the sun rising up into the heavens of the day before me.

You might be wondering why I chose to insert the above picture of a sunrise I saw a few days ago. As I saw the sliver of light in the winter sky during my quiet time of prayer I felt compelled to walk out on the deck. The first thing I noticed was the heavy cloud cover that seemed to press down close to the earth. As I stood there I suddenly realized I had not noticed the heavy black factory smoke rising up almost reaching the clouds. I picked up my camera and tried to take a clear picture, but I could tell it was out of focus. In just a few moments I was in awe as I watched the light from the sun rising higher in the sky. The brilliant glow of deep iridescent crimson mixed with yellow came up behind the black smoke and cast its rays all the way across the cloud cover of the sky. I had just been praying a few minutes earlier; asking God to somehow bring his glory into this world of dark confusion, anger and hatred. It seems this picture, out of focus, very much describes what I have walked through the past few months. I have had other types of situations where my faith grew deeper, but had never suffered a brain injury so this was going to be a new experience in courage. For some time I could not read or write and that can be a frustration for a writer. In the next few weeks, the blessing is that I never had a headache, never felt sad or depressed, but I knew this was not going to be a quick fix.

During my recovery my thoughts were like the photo above, confused and muddled. Fear was not my companion as I could look back over my life and through every trial and hardship I have come to know I could have faith in the assurance the Lord would never leave me alone. Somehow I knew and could feel that down in my subconscious mind and spirit the God of the universe was doing something beautiful.

The amazing realization is that in sickness or conflict, if we have learned the word of God, it comes to us in the night season. I would say this was one of those night seasons for me, as in the weeks to come I would wake again in the night and know Jesus was right there with me.

If I say, "Surely the darkness will hide me and the light
become night around me." even the darkness will not
be dark to you; the night will shine like the day,
for darkness is as light to you. Psalm 139:11- 12   NIV

As I look about me, listen to the daily news and sometimes just turn off the TV, I wonder what I could possibly do in this time of upheaval. I grew up in a community where the fathers were all war veterans of WWII. Patriotism was a very big deal. There were times when the national anthem was played I would see tears in my father's eyes. Gangs seize upon this time of unrest to tear up businesses and make cities, once peaceful, a place of terror. On and on one could lament, as if all common sense has run amuck. And then there is God in all of his glory, loving every living creature regardless of color or race or place in society.

For our struggle is not against flesh and blood, but against the rulers, against the authorities, against the powers of this dark world and against the spiritual forces of evil in the heavenly realms.
Ephesians 6:12 NIV

I cannot say I can explain this term called prayer. Why in the early morning hours do I find myself getting up to watch the sunrise and name all my family members in prayer? Why do I pray for our nation's leaders and the hope for Israel? I just know the Bible assures us that God hears our prayers; he sees the tears when we cry for the hurting, and he loves our worship to him. Why would we pray so fervently, when just like the picture above, we see the darkness and confusion settling down over this nation and over the earth?

The God of this age has blinded the minds of unbelievers, so that they cannot see the light of the gospel of the glory of Christ, who is the image of God.
2 Corinthians 4:4 NIV

I wish I was a better photographer, as this picture below has not caught in full the beauty of the morning sunrise. As I watched the light coming up behind the black smoke and dark cloud cover in the eastern sky my heart was overwhelmed in thinking of God's glory that would come over all the earth and dispel the darkness. In just a few moments the sky was full of light and I realized, the night was over and it was the dawning of a new day. Coming out of this season of recovery I am in awe of the beautiful experience that morning and yes I am challenged to just keep praying.

February 7, 2018

For God, who said, "Let light shine out of darkness," made his light shine in our hearts to give us the light of the knowledge of God's glory displayed in the face of Christ.
2 Corinthians 4:6   NIV

CHAPTER 19

COTTON BALLS IN THE SKY

His favor is for life; Weeping may endure for a night,
But joy comes in the morning.
Psalm 30:5NKJV

Depending on the circumstances of grief, and how deeply the emotions reside on one's heart and soul, there needs to be a reprieve from the busy every

day schedules and routine. For some, they fail to recognize this safety net and the toll in health and emotional stability can come up and take a deep biting wound later on.

I have observed this can be the case many times when a parent has lived a very long life; maybe the last years are consumed with sickness such as Alzheimer's. In some aspects there is relief, but also there is a need for the survivors to give themselves permission and time to reset and be able to grieve over the passing of that loved one.

For those of us who have grieved and possibly in your life circumstance the grieving was severe and life can never be the same, so you have been required to totally reset your life, we ask the question, "Is this process of sorrow ever going to end?"

I want you to scroll back to the top of the page, study the picture and let the title soak in for just a few moments

Here is the story behind the story on this one. I had a camera for a number of years I enjoyed greatly, although I never understand how to download pictures, so it was always a trial and error process. But alas the camera was toast, so I bought another, actually nicer camera the summer of the book tour out in Wyoming. I really did try to learn how to use the camera, but it finally went back on the shelf.

A few weeks ago I knew that I needed another camera, but also knew my budget didn't allow for it, so I went to my closet and pulled down the camera and began once again to read the manual. For us grandma types, we recognize the value of all the tecky stuff with phones, computers and cameras, but it is just so embarrassing to ask those simple questions. Actually, I am sure the younger set snickers behind our backs. But at that same time some do seem to take pleasure in walking us through the baby steps.

So, as you look at my picture of "Cotton Balls" in the sky, it is not perfect, but it is on my computer and I have managed to insert it into my document for you my very special reader friend.

What is so significant about this picture you might ask? I would have to say, "Cotton Balls in the Sky," portrays my life now, after many bouts of grief. There were times when I wondered if I would ever come through the situation. Would I ever be able to laugh that deep resounding exuberance at life and the wonder of it all again; that was the question I pondered.

As I have placed the chapters and topics together for this little book on grief, I thought possibly the "Cups of Prayer," would tie it all together in the last portion, but then several mornings ago, as my little dog, Bezoo and I went out in the early morning for his routine, way out behind the trees, I looked up. It was as if the whole morning sky was filled with God's glory as the deep red and amber light seemed to just glow over the pillow like clouds. I had just worked with my camera the night before. I am sure Bezoo wondered what was the matter with me, as I rushed him back to the apartment and grabbed my camera. I hurried back out to the side of the road and there before me were the white cotton balls in the sky. I was so filled with joy of it all.

I am much aware that this story needs to have a conclusion, as there are other stories of life, many filled with great humor and joy that must be penned. In this little book on grief, there have been times I have been a bit surprised at myself, in those snippets of my own story that were filled with such deep sorrow that I was willing to share. It was a very sad time for me when I moved from my vintage home. I do have pictures of that wonderful old home I loved so well. The beauty in all of it is that I was able to write two of my books while living there. Every great once in a while I drive by that home, never thinking I would ever want to go back.

Oh well what can I say? Last week I wrote a children's story and I really do need to take a picture looking out of the sunroom where I saw the wonderful spider web on the late August morning.

So just maybe one day soon I will be brave enough to go knock on the new owner's door, wish them well and bless them, share with them my joy and how I loved their new home. For you see now, I live in an apartment with Bezoo, surrounded by young couples starting out in life. Often I make them hot cinnamon rolls, just so they will know I care about the little things in life in our little corner of the world.

    Some years ago, in a time of deep sorrow, I had an old family friend who lived nearby. He was well up in his eighties at that time. He would look at me, sometimes when the unwanted weeping would come and say, "I feel so sorry for you." It was almost like a knee jerk reaction for me, as I would respond with, "Oh no, don't feel sorry for me that is a luxury I cannot afford."

    I just had an innate sense that I had to get through that time just as if I was heading into the Wyoming winds. Believe me when I say Wyoming winds can be brutal. Although, the grief at times seemed all consuming, I just had to face the pain of it. Then when the writing began, it truly was as if I found myself saying in the first poem I penned to the page, "This is the first day of the rest of my life."

    I have spoken of these tools of coping in previous chapters, but in closing I find myself going back and looking at the "Cotton Balls in the Sky." The beauty in the picture just causes the tears to come now. Not of sorrow, but of such deep joy, that my life has been so rich and filled with such beauty of soul and spirit.

For I have recognized those qualities of kindness, forgiveness, thankfulness and humility were refined in those times of grief when I knew I so needed a kind and loving heavenly father. And, so throughout my life, it is as if I have been that young child who just ran to her father and let him sweep her up in his arms and hold me tight until the storm passed over.

For I know the thoughts that I think toward you, says the Lord, thoughts of peace and not of evil, to give you a future and a hope.
Jeremiah 29:11NKJV
February 2017

SECTION V

MOSS COVERED FLOWER POTS MADE OF CLAY

CHAPTER 20

BROKEN CLAY POTS

As I go back through my collection of many stories of the flowers on my deck and garden, I come across the picture of the empty flower pots. My favorite of all down through the many years are the two that had an artist's design of simple. The large terra cotta pot looks ancient as the deep hues of sage green moss quietly seep up through the crusted orange texture giving it a look of the old country. I found the two that first spring after I had purchased a wonderful old vintage home with a deck looking out on the backyard.

It has been many years now that I looked forward to what type of flowers would be planted each spring.

I moved from that home into an apartment with a small deck adjacent to my living room with a southern exposure. Although much smaller, I still took great care in how I placed my flower pots and the colors and textures that would be placed in each one. I would have to say coming from the vision of an artist/writer type, textures, colors and dimension are my muse.

At the first of this year I moved into a cottage with an incredible view of the lake. So now my muse would include looking out on the ice covered waters in the beginning that now have thawed. The smaller flower pot broke into many pieces last spring. In moving I had my grandson Reagan very gently bring the larger flower pot up onto the much larger deck with a view looking out on the lake. I placed it inside of another larger flower pot hoping I would have another season of using it as my focal point of artist's design.

That first month I worked long hours every day unpacking boxes and trying to complete the task in every room. This is an old lake cottage with its many repairs that will take time, but needless to say I love this old house with its many windows looking out on the splendor of water.

I think we would all agree that our nation has never experienced a time as we have lived through in the last year. Not just our nation, but all over the world the Covid 19 pandemic has brought with it many deaths, sickness and lockdowns. If I were to use one word to describe what many are experiencing I would have to say "FEAR. "What has complicated the very serious situation is it has become like a political football the media has used to bombard the daily news with conflicting reports until one would ask themselves is there any one left with just some common horse sense.

I have had several bouts with pneumonia and I am on the other side of the middle seventies, so my family has been very protective of me, as we all so hoped I could come through this time without Covid. Well I do remember February 10th. I went to bed with a migraine, sick to my stomach all night and chest pains. I hoped for a few days I just had a bad cold, but that was not going to be the outcome.

I have been in this valley of sickness in the past, and so now I find I must write down those thoughts that are now coming to me as my strength is returning and my thought process is not so muddled. I have written many stories full of joy in my love of flowers but I also have those snippets of life when I would be recovering from sickness or a near death car accident. In those times when I did not now the outcome, there was always that sense of hope and knowing I had a future and this would not be wasted time.

In this season of sickness, I would manage to get up and draw the blinds every morning and look out on the lake. I am thankful for this little cottage and the quietness of it all for as I am gaining strength in the mornings I sit here on the couch and describe the thoughts that come as brooding. These are not sad or fearful thoughts, but more of the anticipation of just how will this great Shepherd of Heaven fill my heart and soul of beautiful thoughts of healing and renewed strength.

So many times when my thoughts come in layers of life, songs from the past come to mind. This morning I looked up "Spirit of the Living God." From what I have gathered I believe this song was written by Daniel Iverson in 1926. That is a long time ago. Several lines from the song describe how my spirit feels in these days of recovery.

> "Spirit of the Living God, fall fresh on me,
> Spirit of the living God, fall fresh on me.
> Melt me, mold me, fill me, use me."

I was finally able to venture out onto my deck a few days ago so of course I wanted to inspect my most cherished flower pot. Well, sad to say, it was in many pieces. In fact, when I picked it up, it seems the terra cotta layers just crumbled. As I looked down on the broken pieces I thought of the scripture I have prayed from the time I was very young.

> *But now, O Lord, You are our father;*
> *We are the clay, and You are our potter;*
> *And all we are the work of Your hand.*
> *Isaiah 64:8 NKJV*

As I observe the troubled times we are living through, I also know that our Father in Heaven never slumbers, is always aware of every situation and his love over mankind never changes. In those days when I felt so ill, I remember looking out on the lake in the mornings, just so thankful of this journey I have had with God I can look back through all these years and remember the outcome of so many experiences where the potter fashioned something so incredible, sometimes from the hard knocks of life.

As I was walking through those days of Covid, I would describe it as a silent time. I was never sad or fearful, just a bit surprised that breathing had become so difficult. There was always that hope of the thoughts that would come in just a short while. So today my cherished friends, who have not heard from me for a while, I just wanted to send a few thoughts and let you know all is well.

CHAPTER 21
POTTER'S HAND

I have to confess to you the reader; it has been one of those mornings. All I can say is that I feel undone. Oh I have been in this place many times. It is not a depressed state that I am in, but rather as I look out on the lake and reflect of these weeks I have been in my cave of writing, I am beyond thankful.

I know there were many times when the residual effects of Covid would bombard my thinking process, and the weariness would set in, I would pray for the Lord to bring angels to lift me up and then I could finish that portion so heavy on my heart for that day.

My grandson Kam and his new wife Kassie, who is beautiful inside and out, had not seen my cottage. I really wasn't that strong yet, but one night had them come to dinner. The broken pieces of the clay pot had been setting there on my deck for at least a week. I kept going out and rearranging the pieces and adding more, although it was difficult as the clay would just dissolve into dust in my hands. By now you are probably saying to yourself, "What is the deal with this old clay pot, broken beyond repair". Oh dear friend I do have an answer. "It is the memories; the good the bad and the ugly, the times of sorrow and then those other days of beauty held in this flower pot that could be added to the ancients.

My grandchildren take great delight in teasing me, which is just fine as each one of them is such a delightful component of my life. Kam and I have always had that special connection And just like always when he looked at the broken pieces of pottery lying there on the deck, he jokingly said, "Well Grandma, how long are you going to leave that broken flower pot setting there?" Well yes, I do need to get on with it. As I studied the picture of the broken pieces in Chapter 20, I then compared it to the picture that was taken years ago that already had layers of green moss, giving it an exquisite and beautiful intricate design. When I compared the two pictures I noticed that the deep green shades of moss had been bleached out those days setting there on the deck in the cool spring mornings.

As you have read through the snippets of stories of my life and recognized how often I have heard the silent voice of God in the times of grief, you might be saying, "But I have never heard that silent voice." I would dare say you are going through your own grief at this point or I doubt that you would be reading to the end of this book. Just like me, that day in a snow storm that had lasted for days, I felt compelled to start my life of writing.

I have often said that was the "first day of the rest of my life." And for you dear friend that I might not ever meet this side of Heaven, that silent voice of the Shepherd of Heaven has been calling you forever so long, so just go to that quiet place in your life and allow God's heart of compassion to touch you in your time of sorrow.

On the other hand, very possibly the reason my heart has been so heavy this morning is I am speaking words of life to you the servant. You are that one who has loved God all your life. You have been a faithful servant spending your life ministering to others, and now your heart is so broken you feel maybe your journey is done. In your time of brokenness, if nothing else remains in your memory of this story, can I say to you, "your journey is not done yet."

The Lord is going to come to you, lift you up, and you will finish well. Keep climbing that mountain, although the winds of adversity are blowing hard against you. Keep walking, saint of God!

I am brought back in memory of that night out in the middle of nowhere in Shirley Basin, Wyoming. The temperature had dipped down to twenty below; the winds were blowing so furiously through the broken windows. I did not have a coat on. It was way in the back seat covered in broken glass.

I had been waiting for the ambulance for over an hour. I knew I did not dare cry. Once again as in past times of adversity there was that silent voice from my father's death bed, "Don't Give up Patty, remember what I said when I was dying, "I'll never give up hope."

I am going to insert here a snippet of story of that time of recovery. I had so many internal bruises, my knees had been badly injured and I was in a great deal of pain, but I was just happy to be alive. I had a sense that the Lord was not ready to bring me home to Heaven and so for you I say with all the compassion and empathy within me, "Don't give up hope dear friend!"

ROBIN RED BREAST

February is winter in Wyoming. The winter sportsman thrives on heavy snows. Shepherds with large flocks of sheep manage to get through the lambing season, and the rest of us hope we can set next to a log fire place in the evenings. And then comes March with a possibility that a few warm and blustery days will let us know winter has almost past.

It was a month after the wreck in Shirley Basin. I was happy to be in my home in Shell. No complaining came from me, as I was grateful to still be here. I knew it was early for spring, but I couldn't help but look out on the trees, hoping to see the first bud of leaves. The surgeon advised waiting to see how my knees would improve before doing surgery. I was surprised that the bruises had not disappeared. My feet were still a dark purple, and I was for the most part house bound. I was filled with high spirits on this morning as I looked into the long mirror, combing my hair.

I had managed to take a shower, what a luxury. Such an ordinary daily process, now took all the energy I could muster. I wasn't discouraged, but the thoughts would come as a question. How would I ever be strong enough to go back to work if this simple task left me so exhausted?

Three picture windows filled the northeast wall of the living room with a view of the west range of the Big Horns Mountains. At times birds would be blinded by the morning sun rays and would fly into the windows.

As I stood there combing my hair my mind was full of questions. What is going on inside of me? Is there something the doctors haven't discovered? Will my life ever come back to normal? As I stood there, I realized I needed to be done, and lay back down. I heard a loud bang. I went to investigate with Timmy, my Yorky type dog at my heels. As I went to the front glass sliding door, I gently pulled it open. I called Timmy back into the living room as he saw it and had quickly gone out on the deck.

There in front of me lay a little Robin Red Breast. Its wing looked broken and I knew the little bird was stunned and in a great deal of pain. My pain had already reached the breaking off zone, so as I looked at the bird there, his eyes fixed on me I felt a great compassion for him. What could I do? I must put him out of his misery. I had no weapons in the house. I limped back into the living room, went to the kitchen drawer and pulled out a hammer. As I came back on the deck, somehow I managed to get down on my knees.

There was no way I was going to be able to hit that little bird. I gently picked the little bird up and cradled him in my hands and began to pray.

"Dear Heavenly Father, you know how much pain I am in, please let me help this little Robin."

He lay very still as I whispered to him, his eyes studying me intently. I laid him back down as carefully as I could and went back into the house. A few minutes later I came back out, anxious for the Robin. To my joy and amazement he was perched up on the railing. As I quietly came out on the deck, my little Robin Red Breast turned his head back and looked at me. He then lifted both wings and up into the blue sky he flew.

God speaks to each of us in such incredible ways. He will use the smallest things to speak profound truths to our hearts when we need it the most. For the rest of the day, I felt peace and my faith was reassured as I spoke over and over, "Just like my little Robin Red Breast, I will fly again.

Patricia, March 2001

"The Lord is my light and my salvation; whom shall I fear?
The Lord is the strength of my life; of whom shall I be afraid?
When the wicked came against me to eat up my flesh,
My enemies and foes, they stumbled and fell.
Though an army may encamp against me,
My heart shall not fear;
Though war may rise against me, In this I will be confident.
One thing I have desired of the Lord, That will I seek:
That I may dwell in the house of the Lord
All the days of my life,
To behold the beauty of the Lord, and to inquire in His temple.
For in the time of trouble
He shall hide me in His pavilion;

> *In the secret place of His tabernacle*
> *He shall hide me;*
> *He shall set me high upon a rock.*
> *Psalm 27: 1-5* NKJV

As I am bringing this book relating to grief to a close, I am well aware that it is only one portion of this life journey that also has layers of beauty of joy and peace. I am glad that from the beginning I dated the poems and stories that have been woven into the narrative. It has not been in chronological order as those experiences that have developed strength and courage seem to surface once again when we are in the throes of grief. I don't think I could put into words how grateful I am this morning as I write that I can look out on the lake and see those swans gliding smoothly through the waters as it brings a peace and calm to my soul.

My family and friends helped me move into my lake cottage the last part of December. Unfortunately, I think it was the worse day of winter. Boxes filled the rooms and there was much to do, so little worker bee that I am I just dove right in and began unpacking.

The large picture windows are drafty right here next to the lake so a few days later my special friends who now are my neighbors, Kelly and Catherine Richmond came over and helped me put heavy plastic on the windows. It mars the view just a bit, but it is a relief as it made a big difference in the warmth in the cottage. I began my garden of flowers on the deck of my home when I lived in Shell, Wyoming. There were four picture windows with a deck wrapping around the home. From every focal point I could see another view of the canyon that looked up into the Big Horn Mountain range.

When I moved from my home in Shell, I left the flower pots with my special friend and neighbor Linda Reed. I was happy a few years later when I came to visit Linda that there setting on the step was the rust colored terra cotta flower pot I had given her.

That first spring after moving to Michigan I bought a wonderful old vintage home with a deck looking out on the back yard with a maple tree that gave shade on the north side of the house. I found the terra cotta clay flower pot along with a smaller size that first spring I lived in my new home.

I never thought that one day the moss colored flower pot, which was my favorite, would someday be the focal point of the last chapter of a book on grief. This picture was taken with all my empty flower pots setting on the deck of the vintage home that spring in 2008 after a long bout of sickness that winter. I managed to focus in on just this one, but if I would have known I would have taken many pictures. Each summer more layers of green moss hues of colored were added to this flower pot blending into the amber colored terra cotta. It became a picture of intricate beauty through the years.

My next deck full of flowers was in an apartment. I became very creative in ways to add shepherd hooks and pottery stands to give height and depth to add more flowers, which by the end of summer would fill up the small space.

Now, I will speak of the cover of this book and of my journey through times of grief that I shared with this little Yorky type dog named Timmy.

Once again, I have to say, in all those eighteen years of loving this little writing buddie of mine, the thought had never occurred to me that one day he would be the main character in this collection of snippets of life.

I refer back to that time in 1986 when my father passed away. I did go through all five stages of grief with his passing and it was not a quick fix. What I have come to recognize throughout this life journey is that nothing is wasted. The deep moss of sorrow has a way of seeping up through those times of joy and beauty, giving life a dimension of rare tranquility.

I remember well the day we received the news that it was discovered our father had cancer of the lungs and it had moved to his liver. He was given from two weeks and at the most five months. My brother Mike and his family were missionaries in Kenya, East Africa, I lived with my family in Detroit, Michigan and Wayne and his wife Pam still lived on the McClaflin farm across the road from the homestead house. Our father passed away in July of 1986. Not long ago Wayne and I were talking about our dad.

He said, "Sometimes it seems like it has been over thirty years, and then on some days it seems like yesterday." I would have to agree with my brother as I miss my father so keenly. Many times in those snippets of life experience he will come into the story. He was such a quiet and gentle man, how could he have ever known how deeply I loved him? When it comes to this emotion we have labeled grief, it comes in many degrees.

The other day when I stopped by the apartment complex to look at that little garden patch for the last time, I saw the rock I had placed on top of Timmy's grave.

I decided to pick it up and bring to my new home at this wonderful cottage on the lake. The grief has passed on to acceptance now of Timmy. As I write and tell the stories of the delightful memories of this little pet I am at peace. I have come to the acceptance stage of grief of the Daddy I love so well, but I will always miss him.

It was about a month after my father had died that I remember I was driving down Telegraph Road in Detroit with a person I considered a very close friend. I was telling her I was still so grief stricken, at times it seemed it was hard to breathe. I was shocked at her angry response, "Are you still grieving, just get over It.?" Unfortunately for me, I felt like maybe I did not have the right to feel grief, so I just shut down and grieved in silence. Looking back on that conversation, later when I was able to think more clearly I came to understand that she did care deeply at my lost, but she had so much of her own brokenness she just could not take on my grief. She passed away several years ago.

It has made me very sad that I was never able to help her walk through her grief that later impacted her life so greatly. I am not speaking here of using grief to manipulate others. What I am saying is in times of grief if we can have a friend walk along side of us with empathy and compassion it can ease the ache in our broken heart.

As I ponder this topic of grief, one of those qualities that can grow out of the experience is a greater awareness of those around us. After the many facets of grief if we can be open to caring about others the quality of empathy and compassion can take on another color of beauty we can share with another.

I would not try and expect this of yourself in the first stages of grief when you are left numb with unbelief and sorrow, but give yourself some time.

Sometimes in this journey we call life that friend that helps us take another step up that steep mountain is like that elderly Asian gentleman that day I was so sad and full of grief as I was going for the biopsy. As he carried my gardenia flower to my car, I felt like he was a kindred spirit. As I shook his hand, the look of kindness on his face gave me the buoyancy and faith to make it through the afternoon. I am thankful the God of Heaven brought him along my path that day.

My mother missed her 100th birthday by just thirty-seven days. There were many times as I was finishing up the homestead book, I would have a question and think, "I need to call Mom," quickly realizing she is in Heaven. I had made a copy of the manuscript one Christmas and sent it to her, but it was not like placing the book in her hands.

What helped me through that time of accepting her death was remembering those months I made the dress she was buried in. It truly was a work of art when it was finished. I see that as the resilient tool that comes from creativity in dealing with grief. As I sewed every bead and made every flower I was walking through the process of telling my mother, who was so precious to me, "Good-by." On those days I missed her so keenly; I would quickly whisper a prayer of thankfulness that she did not have to suffer through the isolation of being locked-down because of Covid. I just could not have wished that for her.

In those silent days and weeks as I walked through the time of Covid this winter, I could remember what it was like after I fell and had the concussion several years ago. I knew I just had to be patient day after day and then slowly I became stronger.

I am thankful for my friend Jessie, who went through a great battle with Covid last year. She would encourage me in those weeks, that yes; I would come out of this time of sickness.

In those first few weeks I could not even think clearly but then those snippets of thoughts began to surface, and I wanted to do my part in this time of upheaval and fear in our nation and around the world. What could this little grandma who had grown up out there on the wind swept plains of northern Wyoming, feeding sick baby orphan lambs, have to say to a hurting world?

I read scriptures in the Bible that say we will leave an inheritance. It can be for good or for evil. All those years I was writing the history and research outcome for "Beloved Homeland," above my desk was a note written out that kept me going with hope. Now in this little cottage on the lake I have the verse printed on a rock setting there on my dining room table.

Ask of Me, and I will give You The nations for Your inheritance,
And the ends of the earth for Your Possession.
Psalm 1:8 NKJV

Hopefully as grandparents, we are that encourager with unconditional love for our families. The role we play with the grandchildren can be invaluable. I have found they have in turn been a great source of strength for me.

Several years ago after the concussion in the early part of December there was a period of time I was too weak to come to church. One Sunday morning my daughter Shana came and picked me up. I sat in the back with her husband. I was so weak and it was hard to think. After church my family and friends gathered around me and prayed. Oh, such beautiful prayers full of faith and courage they prayed over me. My granddaughter Anna stood there with her arm tightly wrapped around my waist. She prayed, "Grandma, you're going to end well. You have loved God and each of us all your life and you will be strong and end your journey well!"

PASSING ON THE BATON

Several years ago I attended a Women of Faith Conference in Billings, Montana with my friend Teddy Jones. What I remember most of those few days, was the one comment made by Sheila Walsh; "Don't die before you are dead." This morning I woke before the dawn of day with the words of the song written many years ago in my thoughts.

Something beautiful, something good
All my confusion He understood
All I had to offer Him was brokenness and strife
But he made something beautiful of my life.

Author: Gloria Gaither, 1971

As I sit here looking out on the ducks gliding smoothly through the cool spring waters, I could say the words were written just for me.

As I scroll down through the table of contents and see the many snippets of stories and tools to walk through those times of grief I am moved to tears knowing the journey up that steep mountain path has been an adventure in resiliency described sometimes as sorrow and in other seasons pure joy of loving and knowing I am loved.

There were times in the process of walking through grief it would be those everyday occurrences that would bring faith and hope. The poem, "Deep Calls to Deep," you find in Chapter 12, was one of those winter times of the soul for me. As I look at my life now, I believe I am in the last part of summer going into harvest time.

The beautiful clay pot that finally broke into many pieces lay there on the deck for some time.

As the morning sun bleached out the deep green colors of moss that had seeped down into the crevices of clay slowly faded and only the bright and cheery amber color remained. That is how I see this season in my journey as the humor, creativity, forgiveness and thankfulness of just pure joy have returned. My family, friends and the swans that come every morning have truly made the experiences of life into something beautiful. The last chapter of the "Beloved Homeland" book is entitled, "Passing on the Baton." In this season of my own journey I find myself in that stage recorded in Erik Erickson's book as "Integrity verses Despair." I can truly say that as we walk out our journey with this amazing Shepherd of Heaven, he does become the Potter who takes all those pieces of the clay, so broken, and fashions a life of beauty.

As I have written the words day after day, my prayer is that you will find that source of strength and faith as you walk through your own time of grieving.

"The Spirit of the Lord God is upon Me,
Because the Lord has anointed Me
To preach good tidings to the poor;
He has sent Me to heal the brokenhearted,
To proclaim liberty to the captives,
And the opening of the prison to those who ae bound.
To console those who mourn in Zion,
To give them beauty for ashes, The oil of joy for mourning.
The garment of praise for the spirit of heaviness;
That they may be called trees of righteousness,
The planting of the LORD, that He may be glorified."
Isaiah 61:1 & 3 NKJV

REFERENCES

Arent, Ruth, M.A., M.S.W., Trust Building with Children Who Hurt. The Center for Applied Research in Education, West Nyack, New York, 1992.

Ayan Jordan, Aha. Three Rivers Press, New York, New York. 1997. Page 259.

Erikson, Erik H. Childhood and Society. W.W. Norton and Company, New York, 1963. Pages 247 – 269.

Kubler-Ross, Elisabeth and David Kessler, On Grief and Grieving. Scribner, New York.

Peck, Scott. People of the Lie. Simon and Schuster, 1983.

Peck, Scott. The Road Less Traveled. Simon and Schuster, New York, 1978.

Seamands, David A. Healing for Damaged Emotions. Chariot Victor Publishing, Colorado Springs, Colorado, 1991.

Westfall, John F., Getting Past What You'll Never Get Over. Revell, Grand Rapids. Michigan, Page 168.

Stoltz, Paul G. Adversity Quotient Turning Obstacles into Opportunities. John Wiley and Sons, Inc. New York, 1997. Pages 18-20.

Wolfelt, Alan D. PhD, Understanding Your Grief. Companion Press, Fort Collins, Colorado, 2003.

Wright, H. Norman, Experiencing Grief. Broadman and Hollman Publishers, Nashville, Tennessee, 2004, Page 84.

BIBLE REFERENCES AND HYMNS

New International Version, NIV

New King James Version, NKJV

"In the Garden," Charles Austin Miles, 1912

"Near the Cross," Francis Crosby, 1869

"O Deep, Deep Love of Jesus," Samuel Trevor Francis, 1875

"Something Beautiful, Something Good," Gloria Gaither, 1971

"Spirit of the Living God," Daniel Iverson, 1926

"Then Jesus Came" Words by Oswald Smith, 1940, Music by Homer Rodeheaver

BOOK ORDER INFORMATION

Patricia and grandson John Booher
Author: Patricia McClaflin Booher weaves a tapestry of life experience, mingled with aspects of creativity, family resiliency and faith in her stories. The outcome brings a sense of time and place across generational lines. She received an M.S. degree in Human Resources, Family and Child Development from Eastern Michigan University.

Book Cover Design by John Booher (Grandson)

To find more information on books and ordering go to:

patriciamac.com and Amazon.com

"Timmy the Timid, Timmy the Tender, Tools for Coping with Grief"
Soft Cover   E-Book
"Beloved Homeland, Growing up on a Wyoming Homestead"
Soft Cover
"Reflections of a Wyoming Shepherd on the 23rd Psalm"
Soft Cover   E-Book   Hardcover

Books to be released in the near future:

"Creativity" Beauty Unfolding
"Lessons of Life I learned in my Garden Patch"
"Here Lamby, Lamby, Lamby

Rock Pavilion Press LLC

"GOD'S BLESSING OF PEACE AND COMFORT TO YOU

IN YOUR JOURNEY"

www.ingramcontent.com/pod-product-compliance
Lightning Source LLC
Chambersburg PA
CBHW051410090426
42736CB00032B/2799